THE VERY VERY
BEST BAD
4-STAR

GENERAL

My journey through contrasting military leadership styles

Major Olly Peter Nyirenda 'psc' ZM

COPYRIGHT

Copyright © 2025 olly.p.nyirenda@gmail.com
ISBN: 978-0-7978-0816-4
All Rights Reserved. No part of this publication may be reprinted or reproduced or utilised in any form or by any electronic, mechanical or other means, known now or hereafter invented, including photocopying and recording, or in any information storage or retrieval system, without permission in writing from the Author.

Warning. The doing of an unauthorised act in relation to copyright work will result in both a civil claim for damages and criminal prosecution.

Published and Printed by
Afrocentric Media House
169 Corobay Corner,
Corobay Avenue
0181 Gauteng
SOUTH AFRICA

1St Print September 2025

FOREWORD

It is with great pride that I write this foreword for The Very Very Best Bad 4-Star General, authored by Major Olly Peter Nyirenda, an officer I have known and observed for many years. I first encountered Major Nyirenda in 2003 at the Botswana Defence Force Academy during the commissioning of officer cadets. To my admiration, he received the Best International Student Award, becoming the first officer cadet from the Kingdom of Eswatini to achieve such a distinction. From that moment, his name was assured of a lasting place in memory.

Since then, Major Nyirenda has earned several awards across defence institutions in the SADC region and within the Umbutfo Eswatini Defence Force (UEDF). Known for his discipline, motivation, and patriotism, he was widely regarded as a reliable officer, teacher, team player, and, indeed, an encyclopaedia for the institution he so faithfully served.

As Commander of the UEDF, I entrusted him with a particularly challenging task: establishing an intelligence unit within His Majesty's Correctional Services. Many had avoided this responsibility, but even during the difficulties of the COVID-19 pandemic, he accepted with courage. By 2021, the unit had been successfully launched under his leadership.

Throughout my tenure, Major Nyirenda worked closely with strategic think tanks within the UEDF. His contributions shaped policy, organisational structures, training, and intelligence coordination, both domestically and regionally. He consistently demonstrated a forward-looking mindset, always committed to strengthening the institution's future.

His intellectual contributions also deserve mention. He authored The Strategic Imperative: National Security and Governance in Monarchical Democracy, which underscored the importance of a codified national security strategy for Eswatini.

Now, with The Very Very Best Bad 4-Star General, he offers both testimony and lessons: a reflection of loyalty, courage, and dedication to the monarchy, the Constitution, territorial integrity, and sovereignty of the Kingdom.

This book is more than personal reflection. It is a mirror for military leaders, a warning against corruption and self-interest, and an inspiration to remain steadfast in integrity and patriotism, even under isolation or injustice. It reminds us that the true measure of a General or any leader is not the stars on the shoulder, but the light of character. I am confident that this work will inspire generations of officers to lead with humility, integrity, courage, and honour.

General Jeffrey Sipho Gubhuzumlambo Tshabalala (Ret.)
Former Commander, Umbutfo Eswatini Defence Force
Mbabane, Kingdom of Eswatini

20 August 2025

PREFACE

Leadership is both a gift and a burden. In every army, every government, and every nation, leaders carry the responsibility to inspire, protect, and serve. Yet, history also reminds us that when leadership falters, the consequences echo far beyond the barracks and the battlefield.

The Very Very Best Bad 4-Star General is not an attack, but a reflection. It is born from lived experiences as a soldier, officer, and student of strategy. The book examines the contrast between great leadership, which uplifts a nation and failed leadership, which erodes morale, weakens patriotism, and threatens unity.

This work is written in service to learning. It is intended to provoke thought, inspire dialogue, and encourage officers, soldiers, and citizens alike to ask difficult questions: What kind of leaders do we follow? And what kind of leaders do we choose to become?

I hope that this book contributes, in its own small way, to the strengthening of patriotism, integrity, and service within our beloved nation States.

DEDICATION

This book is dedicated to my wife, Captain Pholisile Portia Nyirenda, my heart, my anchor through every storm, and my unwavering partner in life's greatest battles. Your loyalty, courage, and love have carried me through the darkest hours. In your strength, I found peace, in your sacrifices, purpose. Without you, none of this would have been possible.

To my children, Thandokwakhe, Abahle, and Abande, you are the light that brightens every shadow and the hope that gives meaning to sacrifice. Your encouragement has been my shield, your laughter my strength, and your innocence my constant reminder of why I must press on. Though you have endured my absence, you have welcomed me with love at every return.

This work is as much yours as it is mine. May it remind every leader that integrity is tested in sacrifice, loyalty is proven in hardship, and the truest command begins at home.

ACKNOWLEDGEMENT

I wish to extend my profound gratitude to His Majesty King Mswati III, Commander-in-Chief of the Umbutfo Eswatini Defence Force, for his steadfast leadership and enduring commitment to the security and prosperity of the Kingdom of Eswatini. His Majesty's unwavering guardianship of our nation remains a beacon of unity and stability. "BAYETHE WENA WAPHAKATHI".

I extend my deepest gratitude to General Sobantu Stanley Dlamini (Ret.), former Commander of the UEDF, for believing in me, mentoring me, and opening opportunities that enriched my knowledge both within Eswatini and beyond.

My appreciation also goes to General Jeffery S. Gubhuzumlambo Tshabalala (Ret.), whose boldness and integrity allowed his story to be told as part of this work. To Brigadier General Zenzele Ace Dlamini, Director of Research and Development, I am indebted to your encouragement and wise counsel. To Lieutenant Tengetile A. Khumalo, UEDF Public Relations Officer, I am grateful for your readiness and courage.

I also thank the generals, officers, men, and women of the UEDF, along with civilian colleagues, whose encouragement and shared memories enriched this book. Special thanks go to Lieutenant Colonel Arthur Phiri of the Zambia Army Public Information Office for his constant support.

To the alumni and faculty of Course 25 of 2023 at the Defence Services Command and Staff College, Lusaka: shoulder to shoulder, we endured the rigours of study and the trials of responsibility. Your resilience and discipline remain an inspiration.

A special word of thanks to my sponsor student, Lieutenant Colonel Patrick S. Chibbonta. His camaraderie and professionalism strengthened my resolve and made this journey possible.

To each of these individuals, I remain sincerely humbled. This book carries the imprint of your guidance, sacrifice, and belief in truth.

> "I salute you all for your loyalty, your courage, and your service. May this work stand as a testament to the enduring spirit of soldiers who never vacillate in duty."

LIST OF ABBREVIATIONS

AI : Artificial Intelligence

BDF : Botswana Defence Force

COLET : College of Education and Technology

D-Day : Day the operation begins

DSCSC : Defence Services Command and Staff College

EI : Emotional Intelligence

FTE : Force Training Establishment

HQ : Headquarters

HUMINT : Human Intelligence

IO : Intelligence Officer

ISIS : Islamic State of Iraq and Syria

PSC : Passed Staff College

PTSD : Post-Traumatic Stress Disorder

SADIC : South African Defence Intelligence College

SADC : Southern African Development Community

SANDF : South African National Defence Force

UAVs : Unmanned Aerial Vehicles

UEDF : Umbutfo Eswatini Defence Force

UGVs : Unmanned Ground Vehicles

U.S. : United States

ZM : Zambia

Table of Contents

FOREWORD 3

PREFACE 5

DEDICATION 6

ACKNOWLEDGEMENT 7

LIST OF ABBREVIATIONS 9

CHAPTER 1 13

THE WEIGHT OF COMMAND 13

CHAPTER 2 19

THE BEST 4-STAR GENERAL: A STUDY OF LEADERSHIP 19

CHAPTER 3 25

THE TRAITS OF A BAD GENERAL 25

CHAPTER 4 30

THE CORRUPT GENERAL 30

CHAPTER 5 41

SUPPRESSING TALENT: THE LEADERSHIP FAILING 41

CHAPTER 6 48

THE MORAL DILEMMA: HATRED, FAVOURITISM, AND THE FALL OF COMMAND 48

CHAPTER 7 54

THE GOOD GENERAL: BUILDING TRUST AND TEAMWORK 54

CHAPTER 8 62

A UNIFIED ARMY: THE STRENGTH OF COLLABORATION 62

CHAPTER 9 69

WHEN SOLDIERS SUFFER: THE CONSEQUENCES OF BAD LEADERSHIP 69

CHAPTER 10 76

LEADERSHIP IN PEACETIME: THE IMPORTANCE OF PREPARATION 76

CHAPTER 11 82

THE LEADERSHIP VACUUM: WHEN GOOD LEADERS ARE GONE 82

CHAPTER 12 90

THE SILENT COST OF POOR LEADERSHIP: INSTITUTIONAL EROSION 90

CHAPTER 13 96

THE PSYCHOLOGY OF LEADERSHIP: THE POWER OF CONFIDENCE VERSUS HUBRIS 96

CHAPTER 14 102

LEADING IN DIVERSITY: EMBRACING STRENGTH IN DIFFERENCES 102

CHAPTER 15 108

ACCOUNTABILITY IN LEADERSHIP: ENSURING TRANSPARENCY AND RESPONSIBILITY 108

CHAPTER 16 117

THE IMPACT OF LEADERSHIP ON CIVIL-MILITARY RELATIONS 117

CHAPTER 17 123

THE ROLE OF TECHNOLOGY AND INNOVATION IN MODERN MILITARY LEADERSHIP 123

CHAPTER 18 129

LEADERSHIP THROUGH CRISIS: MANAGING CHAOS AND UNCERTAINTY 129

CHAPTER 19 136

REBUILDING AFTER FAILURE: LEADERSHIP IN THE AFTERMATH OF DEFEAT . 136

CHAPTER 20 143

THE MORAL COMPASS OF COMMAND: INTEGRITY VERSUS EXPEDIENCY 143

CHAPTER 21 149

TRANSFORMING LEADERSHIP: LESSONS FOR THE FUTURE 149

CHAPTER 22 154

THE FINAL SALUTE – A RECKONING WITH POWER, INTEGRITY, AND ENDURING PATRIOTISM 154

CHAPTER 23 157

WHO WILL LEAD US? 157

AUTHOR BIOGRAPHY 163

CHAPTER 1

THE WEIGHT OF COMMAND

The rank of General embodies more than authority; it carries an immense weight of responsibility and expectation. As the pinnacle of military leadership, a General is entrusted not just with the lives of their soldiers but also with the broader implications of national security, the projection of power, and the safeguarding of a nation's values. It is not merely a rank; it is a profound responsibility that encompasses the lives of countless individuals, the preservation of national interests, and the safeguarding of sovereignty.

A General is the ultimate decision-maker in times of peace and war, and their decisions echo through history, affecting soldiers, civilians, and nations alike. The title carries the weight of expectations, both explicit and implicit, demanding a delicate balance of leadership, strategy, and humanity. The journey to this rank is neither accidental nor casual; it is a culmination of decades of training, operational experience, and an unyielding commitment to service.

Yet, as the title of this book suggests, even those who reach the apex of military command may falter in ways that illuminate the complexities of leadership. To understand the significance of these dynamics, we must first examine the responsibilities and duties that come with being a General and explore the broader nature of military leadership.

THE VERY VERY BEST BAD 4-STAR GENERAL

At its core, the role of a General is to command and lead. This includes the following: planning and executing military operations, developing strategies that align with national objectives, managing vast resources, including human and material.

A General must ensure that the forces are prepared for any eventuality, from combat operations to humanitarian assistance. This readiness requires foresight, meticulous planning, and the ability to adapt to rapidly changing circumstances. Every action must be weighed against potential consequences, both immediate and long-term.

A General's responsibilities are multifaceted and span strategic, operational, and administrative domains. At the strategic level, Generals play a pivotal role in shaping the vision and doctrine of the armed forces. They advise political leaders, participate in crafting national defence policies, and ensure that military objectives align with overarching national interests. This requires not only an astute understanding of geopolitics but also the ability to translate abstract policy goals into actionable strategies.

Their duties also include navigating the complex interplay of politics, diplomacy, and military strategy. In modern warfare, the lines between these spheres are increasingly blurred. A General must work closely with political leaders, often serving as an advisor on matters of national security while maintaining the apolitical stance required of military service. This dual role demands both tact and integrity. Generals must balance the strategic goals of their nation with the realities on the ground. Missteps in this area can lead to catastrophic consequences, including loss of public trust and diminished national security.

Operationally, Generals oversee large-scale missions that often determine the success or failure of entire campaigns. This entails making critical decisions on resource allocation, troop deployments, and engagement strategies decisions that can mean the difference between victory and defeat, and, more poignantly, life and death.

In this capacity, a General must synthesise intelligence reports, anticipate enemy actions, and adapt to rapidly changing circumstances while maintaining morale and cohesion among the forces.

Administratively, Generals manage vast organisational structures. They are responsible for personnel development, ensuring that soldiers are adequately trained, equipped, and cared for. They oversee logistics, manage budgets, and implement policies that affect the day-to-day functioning of the military. Beyond the immediate confines of the armed forces, Generals often engage with civilian stakeholders, whether coordinating disaster relief efforts, fostering international alliances, or participating in public discourse about military matters.

A General's responsibilities also extend to fostering morale, discipline, and cohesion within the ranks. Soldiers look to the General for inspiration and guidance, especially in the most trying circumstances. A General must embody the values and principles of the institution they serve, setting standards that motivate others to follow. Generals are not only military leaders but also mentors and stewards of the next generation of officers. Their ability to cultivate trust and loyalty within their command structure can mean the difference between success and failure.

Furthermore, the role of a General is not without personal sacrifices. The weight of command often comes at the expense of personal time, relationships, and mental well-being. The responsibility for lives lost and missions failed rests heavily on their shoulders, creating an enduring emotional burden. Every decision carries the potential for regret, and the pressure to achieve perfection in an imperfect world can be overwhelming.

The absolute scope of these duties means that a General operates under constant scrutiny. Their decisions are analysed not only by peers and subordinates but also by political leaders, the media, and the public.

The pressure to perform impeccably, coupled with the high stakes of their role, makes the position uniquely demanding and, at times, isolating.

Leadership in the military is both an art and a science. It is rooted in principles refined over centuries, yet it requires a deep personal touch to inspire trust and loyalty. At its core, military leadership is about the ability to influence others to achieve a common goal, often under conditions of extreme stress and uncertainty. For Generals, this means balancing authority with empathy, discipline with innovation, and decisiveness with humility.

One of the defining characteristics of military leadership is its hierarchical nature. The chain of command provides clarity and ensures that orders are executed efficiently. However, effective leadership goes beyond issuing directives; it involves fostering a sense of purpose among subordinates. A good General understands that soldiers are not mere cogs in a machine but individuals with their own aspirations, fears, and motivations. By recognising this humanity, a General can build a cohesive and resilient force capable of overcoming even the most daunting challenges.

Another critical aspect is adaptability. The battlefield is a dynamic and unpredictable environment where plans often unravel in the face of unforeseen circumstances. As the Prussian military theorist Carl von Clausewitz famously observed, "No plan survives first contact with the enemy." Generals must therefore be proficient at thinking on their feet, recalibrating strategies, and leveraging the strengths of their team to seize opportunities as they arise.

Leadership in the military also demands a commitment to ethical principles. While the primary objective of the armed forces is to achieve military success, this must never come at the expense of integrity and honour. Generals are expected to uphold the highest standards of conduct, not only in their own actions but also in the culture they cultivate within their commands.

This includes ensuring compliance with the laws of armed conflict, protecting non-combatants, and treating prisoners of war humanely. Military leadership is deeply intertwined with accountability. Generals cannot afford to shy away from responsibility, whether for the success of a mission or the failures that may occur under their watch. This accountability is not limited to external stakeholders; it extends to the soldiers who place their lives in the General's hands. By embodying a sense of personal responsibility, a General earns the respect and trust of their subordinates, which is essential for maintaining unity and discipline.

While the responsibilities of a General are immense, they also come with a paradox: the higher one rises in the chain of command, the more one relies on others to execute their vision. A General may draft the blueprint for a campaign, but its success ultimately depends on the competence and dedication of countless individuals at various levels of the organisation. This reliance on others highlights the importance of mentorship, delegation, and communication in military leadership. Generals must not only lead but also empower their subordinates to lead in their own right.

In essence, being a General is about managing paradoxes. It is about being decisive yet empathetic, strategic yet adaptive, commanding yet collaborative. This requires an unwavering commitment to duty, an unrelenting pursuit of excellence, and an unshakable sense of purpose. The weight of command is not a burden that everyone can bear. Those who do must possess a rare combination of intellect, courage, and resilience. A General's journey is not defined by successes alone but by the ability to shoulder this immense responsibility with honour and integrity, even in the face of adversity.

This paradox also underlines the fragility of command. A General's reputation can be tarnished by failures not entirely within their control.

Conversely, some may achieve success despite questionable decisions, owing to the strengths of their teams or pure luck. These nuances make the study of military leadership a fascinating yet sobering endeavour, as it reveals both the potential and the limitations of human agency in the face of complex challenges.

The role of a General is both a privilege and a burden. As we delve deeper into this book, we will explore contrasting styles of military leadership and examine how individuals at the highest levels of command navigate the intricate web of responsibilities, relationships, and realities that define their profession. By doing so, we aim to uncover not only what makes a great General but also what can lead even the most promising leaders astray. In understanding the weight of command, we gain insights into the broader dynamics of power, responsibility, and human fallibility.

*

CHAPTER 2

THE BEST 4-STAR GENERAL: A STUDY OF LEADERSHIP

Leadership within the military context is a multifaceted concept that demands a unique blend of traits, skills, and behaviours. A great military leader is defined by the ability to inspire and guide subordinates, an ability usually directed toward achieving strategic objectives under conditions of uncertainty, complexity, and danger. At the core of military leadership lies the capacity to influence others, which is rooted in both formal authority and personal credibility. Key characteristics of exceptional military leaders include, but are not limited to the following:

Visionary Thinking: A great leader conceptualises long-term goals and communicates a compelling vision that aligns with the mission's objectives. Furthermore, a great leader anticipates challenges and adapts strategies accordingly to ensure forces remain prepared for evolving threats. Visionary leaders do not merely react to circumstances; they shape the strategic environment to their advantage.

Decisiveness: Military operations often require swift, informed decision-making, even when complete information is unavailable.

A strong leader maintains composure under pressure and takes calculated risks. This decisiveness is also evident in the ability to delegate effectively to empower subordinates to act with autonomy while maintaining alignment with overarching goals.

Integrity and Moral Courage: Trust and respect are foundational to effective leadership. Leaders must embody ethical principles, displaying honesty and accountability in all actions. Moral courage enables leaders to make difficult decisions, even when they may face opposition or personal consequences.

Empathy and Emotional Intelligence: Understanding and valuing the experiences of subordinates fosters loyalty and cohesion within the ranks. Leaders with high emotional intelligence are adept at recognising the emotional and psychological states of their teams, creating an environment of mutual respect and support.

Resilience and Adaptability: Great leaders navigate setbacks and maintain focus on mission success. They inspire resilience in others through leading by example. Adaptability is particularly critical in fluid and unpredictable combat environments, where flexibility and innovation can mean the difference between success and failure.

Technical and Tactical Proficiency: Mastery of military knowledge and operational expertise enhances credibility and ensures sound decision-making. Leaders who excel in their craft inspire confidence and demonstrate a commitment to professional excellence.

Case Studies

George Washington: *The reluctant commander*

Washington's leadership during the American Revolutionary War demonstrates the power of perseverance and strategic foresight. Despite commanding a poorly equipped and outnumbered force,

Washington's ability to rally his troops and forge alliances was instrumental in achieving independence. His humility and unwavering commitment to the cause earned him the trust of his men and the respect of adversaries. Washington's emphasis on discipline and training transformed a disorganised militia into a formidable fighting force, showcasing the importance of preparation and morale.

Napoleon Bonaparte: *The architect of strategy*

Napoleon's campaigns revolutionised military strategy, emphasising speed, manoeuvrability, and decisive action. His innovative tactics, such as the use of the corps system, allowed for unparalleled operational flexibility. Despite his ultimate downfall, Napoleon's leadership showcased the importance of creativity and boldness in military success. His meticulous attention to detail and ability to inspire loyalty among his troops solidified his reputation as one of history's greatest commanders.

General Dwight D. Eisenhower: *The diplomatic commander*
Eisenhower's leadership during World War II highlights the value of coalition-building and diplomacy. As Supreme Allied Commander, he coordinated a diverse group of nations and personalities to execute the D-Day invasion. His ability to foster collaboration and maintain unity under immense pressure underlines the significance of interpersonal skills in leadership. Eisenhower's calm demeanour and inclusive approach ensured that strategic objectives were achieved without compromising allied cohesion.

General Vo Nguyen Giap: *The master of asymmetric warfare*
Giap, a pivotal figure in the Vietnam War, exemplified the power of strategic patience and psychological warfare. Utilising guerrilla tactics, he successfully countered technologically superior adversaries by exploiting their vulnerabilities and maintaining the morale of his forces. Giap's leadership demonstrated the importance of

understanding an enemy's strategic weaknesses and leveraging the terrain and population in asymmetric conflicts.

A great military leader understands human behaviour and leverages this knowledge to motivate and manage people effectively. Psychological skills essential for leadership include:

- *Emotional intelligence:* The ability to recognise and regulate one's emotions while empathising with others. Emotional intelligence fosters trust and enhances communication within a team.
- *Stress management:* Leaders need to maintain mental clarity and composure under high-stakes conditions. Those who manage stress effectively set an example for their teams and sustain operational effectiveness.
- *Influence and persuasion:* This involves building trust and inspiring confidence in subordinates, peers, and superiors. Great leaders use persuasion to align diverse perspectives and unify efforts.

Strategic leaders possess the ability to see the bigger picture, align resources with objectives, and anticipate potential outcomes. Core components of strategic thinking include:

- *Systems thinking:* Recognising the interdependence of various elements within an operational environment. Leaders who understand these dynamics can prioritise efforts and allocate resources effectively.
- *Scenario planning:* Developing contingency plans for various potential scenarios ensures readiness to adapt to changing circumstances without losing momentum.

- *Risk assessment:* Balancing bold action with prudent risk management. Successful leaders weigh the costs and benefits of their decisions while preparing for unforeseen consequences.

Communication skills: Clear and effective communication is vital in ensuring that objectives, expectations, and intentions are understood across all levels of an organisation. Great leaders tailor their messaging to their audience and utilise both verbal and non-verbal cues to convey confidence and resolve. This communication fosters unity and ensures that every member of the team understands their role in achieving the mission.

Cultural competence: In an increasingly globalised world, cultural sensitivity enhances the ability to work with diverse teams and navigate complex geopolitical landscapes. A leader's understanding of cultural nuances can foster trust and cooperation in multinational operations. Cultural competence also allows leaders to anticipate and mitigate cultural misunderstandings that could undermine mission success.

Decision-making under uncertainty: The fog of war often obscures clarity, making decision-making a critical skill. Successful leaders rely on a combination of intuition, experience, and analytical thinking to make timely and effective choices. Decision-making under uncertainty requires confidence, flexibility, and a willingness to adapt plans as new information becomes available.

While theory and case studies provide valuable insights, the real test of military leadership lies in its practical application. Training and experience are essential for developing the instincts and judgment required for command. Great leaders continuously reflect on their actions, seek feedback, and adapt their approach to meet evolving challenges. Leadership development should emphasise the integration of technical expertise, emotional intelligence, and strategic acumen.

THE VERY VERY BEST BAD 4-STAR GENERAL

The study of what makes a great 4-star general reveals that effective military leadership is a dynamic interplay of personal attributes, strategic skills, and psychological acumen. From Washington's perseverance to Eisenhower's diplomacy, history offers rich examples of leaders who rose to meet extraordinary challenges.

In conclusion, aspiring leaders must cultivate a balance of vision, integrity, and adaptability while committing to lifelong learning and self-improvement. Ultimately, the legacy of a great military leader is not only measured by victories but also by the enduring impact they leave on their institutions and the people they lead. Great leadership transforms individuals, strengthens organisations, and leaves a lasting imprint on history.

*

CHAPTER 3

THE TRAITS OF A BAD GENERAL

In the annals of military history, the most notorious Generals have not always been those defeated in battle, but rather those who eroded the very institutions they were meant to serve. A bad General is often characterised by corruption, nepotism, and self-interest. These three corrosive elements, when combined, can dismantle the effectiveness of an entire military force.

Corruption: *The silent saboteur*

Corruption within military leadership manifests in various ways, from financial mismanagement to the sale of military secrets. A corrupt General prioritises personal enrichment over national security, using their position to siphon resources meant for the welfare of soldiers and operational effectiveness. This corruption is often seen in the misappropriation of funds, where budgets allocated for troop welfare and equipment are misused for personal luxury. Bribery and kickbacks further compromise integrity, with contracts being awarded not to the best suppliers, but to those who offer the highest bribes. Even more alarming is the sale of military intelligence, where critical, classified information is exchanged for personal gain, often compromising national security.

THE VERY VERY BEST BAD 4-STAR GENERAL

The consequences of corruption extend far beyond individual greed. It undermines the morale of troops, who see their efforts and sacrifices squandered by their leaders. Corruption also weakens national defence, as resources meant to ensure readiness are diverted elsewhere. Soldiers under a corrupt General's command are often left under-equipped and demoralised, making them vulnerable in times of crisis.

Nepotism: *Favouring loyalty over competence*

Bad Generals often surround themselves with individuals who are more loyal than capable. Nepotism within the military structure results in the promotion of unqualified personnel due to familial ties, political affiliations, or personal relationships. This practice blocks merit-based promotions, where competent officers are overlooked in favour of those with connections. As a result, a culture of incompetence develops, with key decision-making roles filled by individuals who lack the expertise required for effective strategy and leadership.

The impact of nepotism is devastating. Soldiers and officers lose trust in the chain of command, knowing that promotions are based not on merit but on favouritism. In combat situations, poorly trained and unqualified officers struggle to make critical decisions, leading to unnecessary losses and strategic failures. History has shown that armies led by nepotistic commanders tend to falter, as their internal dysfunction outweighs any external threats they may face.

Self-Interest: *The ego-driven leader*

A bad General is often driven by self-interest rather than the good of the nation or the welfare of their troops. They often seek personal glory, launching military campaigns not out of necessity, but to build their reputation and advance their political ambitions.

Soldier welfare becomes secondary to their image, with decisions made to enhance personal prestige rather than ensuring operational success.

Moreover, self-interested Generals align themselves with political elites, leveraging military influence to maintain their position of power. They prioritise political survival over national security, using the armed forces as a tool for personal and regime security. This short-sighted leadership leads to unnecessary conflicts, loss of lives, and national instability, ultimately damaging the institution they claim to protect.

A bad General does not simply emerge overnight. They develop through a series of destructive behaviours that erode leadership credibility and institutional integrity. These destructive behaviours include the following:

Lack of accountability

One of the most damaging traits of a bad General is their unwillingness to accept responsibility for failures. Instead of acknowledging mistakes, they shift blame to subordinates, refusing to own up to tactical or strategic errors. This behaviour creates a toxic command structure where officers and soldiers fear speaking up, knowing that dissent is punished rather than valued. Without accountability, a culture of fear and stagnation takes root, preventing innovation and improvement in military operations.

Authoritarian rule

While discipline is essential in military leadership, bad Generals enforce rigid and unquestionable authority that stifles independent thought. Soldiers and officers are expected to follow orders blindly, with no room for discussion or alternative perspectives.

THE VERY VERY BEST BAD 4-STAR GENERAL

This suppresses adaptability in battlefield scenarios, where flexible and innovative strategies are often the key to victory. The lack of open dialogue within the ranks leads to poor decision-making, as all critical thinking is centralised in the hands of an incompetent leader.

Disregard for ethical standards

Ethical leadership is the backbone of any effective military, but bad Generals often discard morality in favour of power. They issue unlawful orders that violate human rights and exploit military force for personal political gain. In extreme cases, they engage in war crimes without concern for international law. This unethical behaviour not only tarnishes the reputation of the armed forces but also has long-term consequences, including sanctions, military purges, and loss of international credibility.

Despite their obvious flaws, bad Generals often find themselves in positions of power due to political manoeuvring, opportunism, and systemic failures within military institutions. Several factors contribute to their rise.

These factors include, but are not limited to, the following:

Political favouritism

Many bad Generals ascend to power not through merit but through political patronage. Governments seeking loyal enforcers rather than competent leaders appoint individuals who will serve their interests. This ensures military obedience to the ruling regime, the suppression of opposition forces, and the continued power of corrupt administrations. Such Generals become political tools rather than military professionals, prioritising political survival over national defence.

THE VERY VERY BEST BAD 4-STAR GENERAL

Exploiting crisis situations

Periods of national crisis, whether due to war, economic instability, or political turmoil, create opportunities for ambitious but unqualified individuals to rise to power. They capitalise on fear and uncertainty, presenting themselves as strongmen capable of restoring order. Under the guise of providing stability, they consolidate power through authoritarian measures, aggressive military expansion, or internal purges aimed at eliminating rivals.

Weak institutional oversight

In military structures where oversight mechanisms are weak or compromised, bad Generals thrive. The absence of strong accountability measures allows them to manipulate promotions, suppress whistleblowers, and make decisions without proper checks and balances. Without institutional safeguards, military leadership can be easily hijacked by those who seek personal gain over national security.

In conclusion, the presence of a bad General in military leadership can have devastating effects on national security, troop morale, and overall stability. Their reliance on corruption, nepotism, and self-interest fosters a dysfunctional system where incompetence thrives and accountability is non-existent. Understanding how these Generals rise and operate is crucial for preventing their ascension and ensuring that military leadership remains committed to service, integrity, and national defence. The next chapter will explore how these traits impact military effectiveness, dissecting real-world examples of armies that crumbled under bad leadership and what lessons can be learnt from their failures.

*

CHAPTER 4

THE CORRUPT GENERAL

A corrupt General is the epitome of failed military leadership. This figure, instead of upholding the values of honour, integrity, and duty, prioritises personal enrichment, manipulating military decisions for self-gain and disregarding the well-being of the very soldiers under their command. These Generals do not rise through the ranks solely on merit but often exploit their positions, leveraging political connections, fear tactics, and manipulation to secure and maintain power.

Accepting Bribes: *Selling military integrity for personal gain.*
Bribery is one of the most defining characteristics of a corrupt General. The military is an institution where discipline and loyalty are paramount, but when a leader begins accepting bribes, the very foundation of trust erodes. Bribes may come in many forms: cash payments from contractors looking to secure lucrative deals, expensive gifts from foreign entities seeking military influence, or political favours that compromise the autonomy of the armed forces. The consequences of such corrupt practices are catastrophic. Military resources, meant to enhance operational effectiveness, are diverted into private accounts.

Soldiers find themselves lacking adequate supplies, from basic necessities like food and medical supplies to critical combat equipment. Corrupt Generals often prioritise personal wealth over defence readiness, leading to weakened security and increased vulnerability to both internal and external threats.

Manipulating Orders: *A strategy of deception*

A corrupt General does not hesitate to manipulate orders for personal or political gain. Military decisions, instead of being guided by strategy and necessity, become tools for maintaining power, punishing enemies, and enriching allies. Orders may be altered to favour political elites, delay or fast-track military operations depending on financial incentives, or even redirect forces to serve private security interests instead of national defence. One of the most insidious aspects of order manipulation is how it compromises battlefield effectiveness. Soldiers rely on clear, ethical directives to execute operations efficiently. However, when a General distorts these orders to suit personal interests, it creates confusion, lowers morale, and leads to unnecessary loss of life. In some extreme cases, corrupt Generals may even sacrifice strategic positions or military gains in exchange for financial kickbacks from enemy forces or third-party stakeholders.

Disregarding the well-being of soldiers

A military leader's foremost duty is to ensure the welfare of their soldiers. This duty encompasses proper training, adequate resources, and moral leadership. However, a corrupt General sees their troops as mere tools for personal gain, showing blatant disregard for their safety, mental health, and overall well-being. This neglect is evident in various ways: soldiers are deployed into conflict zones without proper equipment, medical care is insufficient or inaccessible due to misappropriated funds, and veterans are left to fend for themselves without adequate post-service support.

The psychological toll on soldiers serving under a corrupt command is profound. Seeing their sacrifices belittled by a leader who indulges in luxuries while they suffer fosters resentment, disillusionment, and, in extreme cases, insubordination or desertion.

Corruption at the top of a military hierarchy is rarely an isolated issue. Once a General engages in unethical behaviour, it often trickles down through the ranks, poisoning the integrity of the entire institution. Junior officers and enlisted personnel observe their leaders' corrupt practices and either emulate them for self-preservation or resign themselves to a system they believe cannot be changed. This chain reaction manifests in multiple ways:

- *Bribery becomes standard practice:* If high-ranking officials accept bribes, it encourages lower-ranking officers to do the same. Soldiers may be forced to pay for promotions, assignments, or favourable postings. This turns the military into a *pay-to-play* system rather than a *meritocracy*.
- *Lack of accountability:* When a corrupt General goes unpunished, it sends a message that wrongdoing carries no real consequences. Officers who might have resisted unethical practices lose motivation to uphold ethical standards.
- *Erosion of discipline and efficiency:* Once corruption spreads, military effectiveness declines. Soldiers no longer follow orders with conviction, knowing that leadership is self-serving rather than mission-oriented.
- *Increased vulnerability to external threats:* A compromised military is an ineffective military. Corruption weakens national security, making the country susceptible to both internal instability and foreign aggression.

THE VERY VERY BEST BAD 4-STAR GENERAL

Personal Stories

Behind every corrupt General, there are countless soldiers who suffer the consequences. Their stories reveal the true cost of compromised leadership.

Private Maseko: *Betrayed by Command*

Private Maseko was a dedicated soldier who joined the military out of a deep sense of duty to his country. However, his first deployment exposed him to the harsh reality of military corruption. His unit was sent into a combat zone with outdated weapons and insufficient supplies, all because funds meant for equipment upgrades had been funnelled into the pockets of high-ranking officials.

Maseko and his comrades found themselves outgunned and outnumbered. Casualties mounted as they struggled to hold their position. When reinforcements failed to arrive due to logistical failures engineered by corrupt leadership, Maseko recognised that their lives were expendable to those in power. Disillusioned, he left the military, carrying scars not just from battle but from betrayal by his own leaders.

Lieutenant Doctor Ndumiso Dlamini: *Abandoned by Command*
Lieutenant Dlamini was the only dental specialist in the defence force, a quiet professional who brought rare and essential expertise to military healthcare. Trained to the highest standards and committed to the well-being of soldiers, he became a trusted figure among personnel who relied on him for ongoing treatment, recovery, and relief from chronic dental conditions. His clinic became a place not just for medical care, but for compassion and consistency.

However, Lieutenant Dlamini's commitment to his patients clashed with the ambitions of a senior General. This General was more concerned with ticking boxes and flaunting authority than recognising operational needs.

THE VERY VERY BEST BAD 4-STAR GENERAL

The General ordered Dlamini to attend a course unrelated to dentistry, one that would have taken him away from his clients for months. This disrupted crucial treatment plans and left many soldiers in pain or without care. Lieutenant Dlamini respectfully declined. He presented clinical records, patient schedules, and even suggested alternative training more relevant to his field, but logic fell on deaf ears.

The General, wounded by what he perceived as insubordination, turned vindictive. Pressures mounted. The working environment turned hostile. Dlamini was denied support, discredited in meetings, and cornered into making a painful decision: to resign or face further humiliation. He chose to walk away with dignity. His departure left a gaping hole in the military medical force. Soldiers who had begun treatment were referred to civilian hospitals with long queues and high costs. The continuity of care was broken. The morale of medical personnel dropped as they watched one of their best driven out for standing by professional ethics.

The forced resignation of Lieutenant Dlamini exposed how ego-driven decisions by senior commanders can sabotage the very institutions they are meant to protect. The military lost not just a skilled dental specialist but a symbol of integrity and care. The vacuum left behind remains unfilled, creating an ongoing burden on service delivery and diminishing trust in the system. His story is a reminder that when expertise is cast aside for power plays, it is the soldiers, and ultimately the nation, who pay the price.

Captain Dlamini: *Speaking Out Against Corruption*

Captain Dlamini was a promising young officer who refused to turn a blind eye to corruption within the ranks. He witnessed contracts being awarded to companies that supplied substandard gear and saw his fellow officers pressured into silence. Dlamini attempted to report the corruption to higher authorities, only to find himself demoted and reassigned to a remote outpost as punishment for his honesty. His story is a stark reminder that in corrupt systems, whistleblowers are seen as threats rather than assets. Despite his setbacks, Dlamini continued to advocate for reform, using his experiences to expose the widespread corruption that had infiltrated the armed forces.

Major Olly Peter Nyirenda: *Crushed by Corruption, Honoured by None*

Major Nyirenda was the kind of officer every defence force dreams of: disciplined, innovative, and relentlessly committed to service. Over the years, he consistently outperformed his peers in every new task assigned to him. From strategic planning to operational coordination, he delivered results that earned him admiration across the ranks and beyond the borders of his nation. His most celebrated achievement came when he was seconded to a sister security institution to help establish its intelligence unit. Against all odds, and with limited resources, he laid a foundation that remains functional today. Ironically, many of the officers he trained at that prestigious institution and his organisation now outrank him; some are lieutenant colonels, colonels, and others brigadier generals. Yet Major Nyirenda remained stuck in the same rank for more than eight years, while within just twenty months, a lieutenant who was once a corporal that he had trained rose to brigadier general.

  This irony was not the end of his humiliation. He was, at times, elevated to senior appointments only to be downgraded into junior positions. Sometimes he was left without an office or even transport to reach his place of duty. Yet in this wilderness of isolation, he worked from his own home, producing documents of national importance. Through consultations with Generals, he authored a comprehensive operational order, the only one of its kind that was signed by the Commander and distributed across the entire Defence Force. This equipped his country with a defensive plan against potential adversary threats.

Though the plan bore the Commander's signature and prestige, its author remained unrecognised, his name erased from the credit of history.

Even under persecution, Major Nyirenda pressed on. Together with one respected General, he championed the first-ever exhibition of the Defence Force at the Eswatini International Trade Fair. He proudly presented the force to the public and to the region. However, the following year, the military was unable to participate because the very officers who had made the first appearance possible were sidelined, becoming victims of hatred, favouritism, and a perverted system where merit was punished and mediocrity rewarded.

The persecution grew darker. Whispers of slander followed him. One senior General, known for wielding traditional beliefs as instruments of fear, accused Nyirenda of bewitching him to block his success. Another vile rumour claimed, without evidence, that he had leaked an obscene nude video involving a junior female officer sharing the same surname as the General. No disciplinary hearing was held; no proof was ever produced. Yet the mud stuck, and the institution, paralysed by corruption, favouritism, and cowardice, turned its back on him.

Internally, Major Nyirenda bore the weight of betrayal. The silent war waged against him left him with a mild stroke, followed by long months of psychological therapy. Still, he carried himself with dignity. To his peers, subordinates, and foreign counterparts across the SADC region and beyond, he remained a respected strategist, a man of integrity and quiet strength. Many saw the excellence in him which his own Generals refused to acknowledge.

His career was deliberately stalled, his reputation tainted, and his health impaired. Yet worse than all, his loyalty and merit were twisted into crimes he never committed, leaving scars no medal could heal. His family endured the silent suffering, watching a father, husband, and provider stripped of recognition, denied fair advancement, and left in a professional wilderness.

The very household that should have basked in his triumphs bore the burden of his persecution.

The Defence Force crippled itself. By discarding merit and crushing innovation, it lost one of its finest operational minds. It showcased brilliance at the Trade Fair once, then vanished the next year because envy devoured the very officers who made it possible. It adopted an operational plan authored by the Major yet hoburied the author. In silencing him, the institution silenced its own growth. When meritocracy is destroyed, the ripple effects touch the nation's security and its future. By sidelining excellence, the defence force postures weakness. A country's resilience lies not in weapons alone, but in the men and women who can think, plan, and adapt. That capacity was deliberately stifled. The nation now carries the consequences of leadership that confuses loyalty to individuals with loyalty to the state.

Major Nyirenda's story is not only one of betrayal but also of resilience in the wilderness. It is the testimony of a soldier who delivered victories even when stripped of office, transport, and recognition. It is shameful evidence of how hatred and favouritism at the top can corrode the very pillars of national defence. It is also a warning that when a system punishes merit and rewards mediocrity, the nation itself pays the price.

Brigadier General Zenzele Ace Dlamini: *Silenced by Command* Brigadier General Dlamini was a highly respected officer, known for his integrity, professionalism, and unwavering loyalty to the crown and constitution.

Having served his country with distinction for decades, he rose through the ranks not by favour, but by merit, becoming a symbol of patriotism and discipline within the military ranks. His principled stance and refusal to be part of the inner circle of corrupt Generals made him a threat to the high command.

THE VERY VERY BEST BAD 4-STAR GENERAL

One early morning, while on our way to a confidential meeting with officers to address growing concerns of morale decline and abuse of power in the upper ranks, Brigadier General Dlamini was ambushed by twelve armed soldiers in plain clothes. These soldiers, with masked faces and driving three vehicles, intercepted his vehicle, forcefully removed him, insulted him, and confiscated all his communication devices. They held him incommunicado for hours without explanation, denying him access to legal counsel or the opportunity to contact his family or superiors.

It later emerged that the operation had been sanctioned unofficially by powerful figures within the high command. There was fear that Dlamini's increasing popularity and vocal stance against corruption, nepotism, mismanagement, and internal abuse could threaten their hold on power. The event sent shockwaves through the ranks. Soldiers whispered about it in hushed tones. Junior officers watched in fear, realising that even the highest-ranking and most respected among them could be silenced at will. Externally, the story leaked, first as a rumour, then as a scandal, tarnishing the image of the organisation as a professional and lawful defence institution.

The kidnapping of Brigadier General Dlamini by his own comrades, allegedly under orders of corrupt senior officers, marked a dark turning point in the military's ethical fabric. It undermined the rule of law within the institution, fostered a climate of fear and mistrust, and severely damaged the military's public image both at home and abroad. Once hailed as a beacon of professionalism, the organisation now stood accused of silencing its own heroes to protect the egos and interests of a decaying command structure.

The betrayal of Brigadier General Dlamini became a symbol of everything that was going wrong in a once-proud military.

The fate of Brigadier General Dlamini was spoken of in hushed tones, a battlefield lesson that integrity itself could be ambushed. His abduction and silencing became a case study in the decay of institutional ethics.

His silencing by comrades was more devastating than enemy fire, proving that loyalty to corrupt masters now outweighed loyalty to the crown. For the soldiers who once drew strength from his example, his absence cut deep, leaving behind fear where courage once stood.

The betrayal of such a principled leader was not merely the downfall of one man, but the extinguishing of hope across the ranks. It revealed the decay of institutional ethics, where law gave way to brute force, and patriotism was replaced by survival. Internationally, allies began to question the credibility of the defence force as a professional partner, while at home, the people saw in Brigadier General Dlamini's fate the clearest sign that their army had turned against itself, becoming protectors of privilege instead of protectors of the nation.

The long-term consequences of corrupt generals

The effects of corruption in military leadership extend far beyond the tenure of a single General. The long-term consequences include:

- *Weakened national security:* A corrupt military leadership results in a defence force ill-prepared for real threats.
- *Erosion of public trust:* Citizens lose faith in their armed forces when they see them being exploited for personal gain.
- *Loss of international credibility:* Allies hesitate to support nations with corrupt military structures, limiting diplomatic and strategic partnerships.
- *Economic drain:* Corrupt Generals waste public funds, reducing economic investment in genuine defence initiatives.

The corrupt General is more than just a bad leader. They are a liability to the soldiers, the nation, and the integrity of military service. Accepting bribes, manipulating orders, and neglecting the welfare of troops create a cycle of inefficiency and dishonour that erodes both morale and security.

The corruption seeps into the lower ranks, creating an armed force that is more focused on self-interest than duty. The true victims are the soldiers who put their lives on the line, only to find themselves abandoned by those entrusted with their command. The fight against corruption in military leadership requires accountability, transparency, and the courage of those willing to stand against unethical practices. Without these, the institution meant to protect the nation will instead become its greatest weakness.

*

CHAPTER 5

SUPPRESSING TALENT: THE LEADERSHIP FAILING

The strength of any military force lies not only in its numbers but in the expertise, intellect, and innovation of its officers and specialists. A well-led army thrives on the capabilities of its most talented individuals, strategists, engineers, medical personnel, and intelligence officers who contribute to its operational effectiveness. However, bad Generals, often driven by insecurity, arrogance, or political motivations, tend to suppress such talent rather than cultivate it. This chapter explores the various ways in which bad military leadership stifles brilliance, the dangers of dismissing experts, and real-world cases where professional soldiers were silenced under poor leadership.

One of the most common traits of incompetent Generals is their inability to tolerate competition, even when it comes from within their own ranks. These Generals see intelligence and expertise as threats rather than assets. This leads them to systematically suppress officers and specialists who could challenge their authority or expose their incompetence. Talented officers often face deliberate obstruction when attempting to implement strategic innovations or reforms.

THE VERY VERY BEST BAD 4-STAR GENERAL

In an environment where *LOYALTY IS VALUED OVER COMPETENCE,* those who suggest new tactics, criticise flawed strategies, or push for efficiency are often sidelined, reassigned to obscure positions, or forced into early retirement and resignation. This suppression leads to stagnation within the ranks, as innovation is stifled and outdated methods persist.

Moreover, bad Generals often surround themselves with sycophantic officers who are more concerned with maintaining their positions than with the effectiveness of the military. This creates an echo chamber where only agreeable voices are heard, and dissent, no matter how constructive, is punished. The result is a culture of mediocrity where talented individuals either conform or are forced out, leaving behind an institution that is ill-equipped to adapt to modern warfare challenges.

A competent military requires a diverse range of experts to ensure operational success. Doctors, engineers, and intelligence officers play critical roles in keeping an army functional, healthy, and well-informed. However, bad Generals often fail to recognise the importance of these specialists, leading to disastrous consequences.

Medical professionals are essential for maintaining the physical and mental well-being of soldiers. In combat, battlefield medics and military doctors provide life-saving care, preventing minor injuries from turning fatal and ensuring rapid recovery. Furthermore, mental health specialists play a crucial role in addressing post-traumatic stress disorder (PTSD) and other psychological conditions. A bad General who dismisses or underfunds these experts puts the lives of their troops at risk, leading to increased preventable casualties, lower morale, and long-term consequences like increased rates of depression and suicide. History is filled with instances where poor medical support resulted in needless loss of life.

Military engineers are equally pivotal, responsible for constructing fortifications, clearing obstacles, and ensuring supply routes remain intact. In modern warfare, they also design and maintain sophisticated equipment. A General who disregards this expertise places their forces at a severe tactical disadvantage. Poorly prepared battlegrounds, faulty machinery, and inadequate logistical support can turn the tide of war against them. Many historical battles have been lost due to neglected engineering considerations.

Perhaps one of the most critical aspects of modern warfare is intelligence gathering and analysis. Intelligence officers provide vital information that can mean the difference between victory and defeat. Without timely and accurate intelligence, military leaders are forced to make blind decisions. However, bad Generals often ignore or even punish officers who present inconvenient truths, preferring illusions of superiority over reality. When intelligence is ignored or manipulated for political reasons, it leads to catastrophic failures such as misguided invasions, unexpected ambushes, and wasted resources.

Beyond the battlefield, dismissing experts weakens military innovation and long-term sustainability. Scientists and research specialists contribute to the development of advanced weaponry, communication systems, and cybersecurity measures. In an era where technology defines military superiority, a leader who undermines expertise in these fields dooms their forces to obsolescence.

The dismissal of experts extends beyond ignorance; it is often rooted in arrogance and political manoeuvring. Some bad Generals feel threatened by highly skilled officers who challenge their authority or propose innovative ideas. Rather than fostering an environment of progress, these Generals view specialists as rivals, sidelining or outright removing them from key positions. This toxic culture discourages talented professionals from joining or remaining in the military, further diminishing institutional strength over time.

Ultimately, a military force that suppresses or dismisses its experts is one that is destined to fail. Wars are not won through brute force alone but through a combination of strategy, technology, and specialised knowledge. A competent General recognises that true leadership involves leveraging the skills of those around them to ensure that every facet of military operations is optimised for success.

Case Studies

In military service, where integrity, competence, and courage should be rewarded, a silent tragedy unfolds as fear quietly replaces morale. This chapter draws attention to real cases where professional, dedicated, and talented soldiers were stifled, punished, or cast aside not because of wrongdoing, but because they dared to challenge mediocrity, raise concerns, or simply outshone insecure leaders.

For ethical and protective reasons, the names of the states and individuals involved in these accounts have been deliberately withheld. Nonetheless, the authenticity of these case studies has been thoroughly verified. These are the lived experiences of men and women who served with distinction, only to become casualties of a leadership culture that feared dissent more than failure. By examining these stories, we uncover the dangerous consequences of leadership that prioritises loyalty to self over loyalty to the mission and state, and ego over excellence.

Case Study 1: *The Fall of a Brilliant Tactician*

Lieutenant Colonel (a pseudonym), a highly skilled tactician and senior officer, possessed a rare talent for operational planning. His innovative strategies were rooted in modern warfare doctrine and enriched by joint SADC training. If applied, his methods could have greatly improved battlefield coordination and saved many lives. Despite his impressive record, he was systematically sidelined.

His superiors, threatened by his rising influence, dismissed his ideas without review. Their reasoning was rooted in personal dislike for his assertive nature and refusal to participate in corrupt and nepotistic systems.

On one critical occasion, his proposed strategy for a peacekeeping intervention approved by foreign advisors was rejected without justification. Instead, outdated tactics led to confusion, avoidable casualties, and a humiliating failure. The senior officer's warnings had gone unheeded. In the aftermath, his career stagnated, and he was transferred to a non-influential role, effectively silencing one of the nation's brightest military minds.

This case illustrates how progress is halted when leadership is guided by insecurity and favouritism rather than merit. The silencing of this officer not only compromised the mission but sent a chilling message: *"EXCELLENCE IS A THREAT IN A CORRUPT SYSTEM"*. The long-term cost includes the loss of strategic innovation and professional morale.

Case Study 2: *The doctor who warned of a health crisis*

A respected medical officer raised the alarm about a rapidly spreading viral infection affecting soldiers at a military barracks in late 2019. He noticed unusual clusters of respiratory illnesses and immediately compiled a risk report with a containment strategy, including quarantine protocols. However, the General Officer Commanding dismissed the report as alarmist, fearing it would "embarrass the force" before an upcoming delegation.

The medical officer was accused of causing panic and insubordination. No action was taken until it was too late. Within weeks, hundreds of personnel fell ill, some requiring intensive care, and a few fatalities occurred from preventable complications.

Troop morale plummeted, and operational readiness was compromised. Despite being proven right, the medical officer was quietly transferred out of the medical corps, effectively ending his career.

This stands as a tragic example of how denial and authoritarian leadership lead to preventable disaster. The defence force lost a capable doctor and undermined trust in its healthcare systems, creating a chilling effect that discourages others from raising concerns.

Case Study 3: *The intelligence officer who saw the enemy coming*

In early 2021, a skilled intelligence officer submitted urgent briefs warning of an impending cross-border insurgent threat. His analysis, drawn from multiple sources, was clear and credible. He advised reinforcing border platoons and increasing surveillance. Instead of prompting action, the General Officer Commanding the region ridiculed the report, calling it "an exaggerated thesis from a paranoid junior officer" and accused the officer of trying to embarrass him.

A month later, a coordinated nighttime raid on a forward operating base killed one soldier, wounded others, and destroyed critical equipment. The attack, which could have been prevented, shocked the nation. Despite his correct warning, the intelligence officer was sidelined, transferred to a non-operational desk role, and stripped of his responsibilities.

This case is a chilling reflection of how military institutions punish foresight that challenges fragile egos. By dismissing intelligence, leadership failed to prevent a deadly attack and discouraged others from speaking truthfully. It reveals a dangerous institutional malaise where the cost of being wrong is paid in lives.

Suppressing talent within the military is one of the gravest leadership failings a General can commit. The deliberate sidelining of brilliant officers and specialists results in institutional stagnation, strategic failures, and the unnecessary loss of lives. Military success is not solely dependent on raw manpower or weaponry but on the expertise and ingenuity of those who serve.

Leaders who fail to recognise and nurture talent ultimately weaken their own forces and jeopardise national security. A strong military must be built on a foundation of merit, where competence is rewarded, expertise valued, and dissenting but constructive voices are heard. Suppressing talent for personal or political reasons does not just harm individuals; it weakens the entire institution. Moving forward, military institutions must ensure that their best and brightest are given the space to lead, innovate, and contribute, rather than being pushed into silence by insecure and incompetent leaders.

*

CHAPTER 6

THE MORAL DILEMMA: HATRED, FAVOURITISM, AND THE FALL OF COMMAND

In the world of military leadership, there exists an unspoken code of conduct, a moral compass by which commanders should steer their decisions, actions, and attitudes. When a leader's moral compass is compromised by prejudice, hatred, or favouritism, it undermines integrity, weakens cohesion and morale, and threatens the unit's effectiveness. The tragic downfall of a commander often begins with the quiet erosion of these core principles. This chapter explores how these moral failures, hatred, favouritism, and prejudice undermine unity within a military structure and inflict long-lasting damage to military cohesion.

Prejudice and Hatred: *The quiet destroyers of unity*

Unity is the cornerstone of military strength. It is what allows soldiers to function as a seamless unit, working together toward a common objective despite individual differences in background, personality, or perspective. A military leader, entrusted with guiding diverse individuals, must actively preserve and enhance this unity. However, when a commander's personal prejudices take hold, the unity of the entire unit is at risk.

Hatred, whether explicit or subtle, spreads quickly through the ranks, infecting the atmosphere with distrust, division, and tension.

Prejudice and hatred are insidious forces that can slowly undermine the trust between soldiers and their leaders. A commander who allows these emotions to influence decisions inevitably fosters an environment where loyalty is questioned and respect for authority diminishes. This can begin with small, seemingly inconsequential actions: a biased assignment, a dismissive attitude toward certain individuals, or a deliberate exclusion from opportunities. Over time, such actions compound, creating an atmosphere where soldiers no longer see themselves as equals. Instead, they see themselves as individuals marked for either inclusion or exclusion based on characteristics beyond their control, such as race, religion, ethnicity, or political affiliation.

The fallout from a commander's prejudice is not confined to the targeted individuals. The corrosive effects ripple outward, affecting the unit as a whole. Soldiers who observe their peers being marginalised, mistreated, or unjustly punished develop a sense of betrayal. When soldiers lose faith in the integrity of their leadership, they begin to disengage. Their commitment to the mission, to their fellow soldiers, and even to their own personal sense of duty starts to erode.

The bond that holds soldiers together is broken, replaced by a culture of fear, division, and suspicion. The very foundation of military strength and unity begins to crumble. In the worst cases, this mistrust and division can spread so far that the commander's authority is no longer respected, leading to insubordination, defiance, or even rebellion.

The long-term impact of a commander's hatred and prejudice can extend well beyond the immediate effects of a particular decision or incident. It leaves scars on the culture of the military unit. Soldiers who are subjected to or witness such behaviour may internalise the same prejudices, perpetuating a cycle of division that can be difficult to break.

Moreover, the external perception of a unit led by a commander with such moral failings can suffer significantly. Public trust in the military is not only about how the military performs in combat; it is also about how it treats its own. When an institution is seen as fostering a climate of hate, it loses the moral high ground necessary to inspire confidence from both the public and its allies.

Favouritism: *The dangerous costs*

While prejudice and hatred are explicit forms of bias that openly damage unity, favouritism operates in a more subtle, yet equally destructive, manner. It is often less overt than hatred, but its consequences are just as far-reaching. When a commander shows preferential treatment toward certain individuals or groups based on personal relationships, shared backgrounds, or other irrelevant factors, it undermines the principle of fairness, which is essential to maintaining military cohesion. Soldiers who feel overlooked or unfairly treated begin to question the integrity of the system.

Favouritism can manifest in numerous ways; it may be seen in promotions, assignments, or the distribution of opportunities. A soldier may receive favourable treatment because they are close to the commander, share a similar background, or have ingratiated themselves with those in power. The favoured individual may be given preferential assignments, access to resources, or opportunities for advancement.

THE VERY VERY BEST BAD 4-STAR GENERAL

In contrast, those who do not fall within the favoured group may feel sidelined, regardless of their skill, dedication, or contribution to the unit. The failure to reward merit and dedication leads to a breakdown in morale and a decrease in motivation. Soldiers who feel their hard work and capabilities are not being recognised are less likely to put in the effort required for success.

In the long run, favouritism not only breeds resentment but also sabotages the meritocratic principles that are fundamental to any effective military unit. A military organisation that bases advancement on favouritism rather than merit risks undermining its operational effectiveness. When soldiers who are less qualified or less experienced are promoted over those with proven track records, the unit's overall competence declines. Soldiers who are deserving of leadership positions but are passed over due to favouritism may become disillusioned, feeling that their efforts are in vain. They may lose confidence in their abilities, and their commitment to the unit will falter.

Favouritism also fosters division within the ranks. It creates an environment in which soldiers align themselves with certain individuals or factions, leading to a fragmented unit. As soldiers begin to pick sides, the unity that is essential to success begins to erode. This internal fragmentation weakens the collective purpose of the unit. When soldiers are divided along lines of favouritism, loyalty to one another and the command structure weakens. In such a setting, it becomes increasingly difficult for the commander to maintain control, and the cohesion of the unit begins to suffer. This weakening of unity makes the unit more vulnerable, both in day-to-day operations and in combat situations.

The most damaging effect of favouritism is that it erodes the trust soldiers have in their leadership. Trust is the bedrock upon which military success is built. Soldiers must believe in their commander's ability to make decisions that are in the best interest of the unit, not based on personal relationships or biases. When favouritism becomes apparent, trust in leadership begins to crumble. Soldiers may begin to question the fairness of orders, the motivations behind decisions, and the integrity of the command structure. A loss of trust is devastating to military morale. Soldiers who do not trust their leadership will not fight with the same commitment or discipline. They will not perform at their best, and they may even undermine the efforts of others. In a military unit, the breakdown of trust can have catastrophic consequences.

The Fall of the Commander: *The inevitable consequence*

The damage caused by prejudice and favouritism eventually becomes too much to ignore. The cost is paid not only for the loss of military cohesion but also for the fall of the commander who allowed these moral failings to flourish. When a commander's leadership is rooted in hatred or favouritism, it becomes increasingly difficult for them to maintain the respect and loyalty of their soldiers. The very qualities that made them successful leaders in the past, the ability to inspire trust, unity, and a sense of shared purpose begin to unravel.

As the unity of the unit collapses, so does the commander's authority. Soldiers who feel isolated, overlooked, or unjustly treated will no longer follow the commander's orders with the same level of dedication. The commander may face resistance, disobedience, or outright defiance. Soldiers may begin to question the legitimacy of the commander's leadership, and the commander's influence over the unit may weaken. In extreme cases, this can lead to a complete breakdown in discipline, with soldiers refusing to obey orders, undermining the effectiveness of the unit in critical moments.

THE VERY VERY BEST BAD 4-STAR GENERAL

The loss of respect and loyalty from soldiers is compounded by the fact that the commander's actions will often come to the attention of higher-ranking officers or military leadership.

The commander's ability to lead effectively will be scrutinised, and their career may be in jeopardy. At this point, the fall of the commander becomes unavoidable. A leader who has separated their soldiers, undermined unity, and violated the core principles of military ethics is no longer fit to lead. Their once-promising career, built on skill, experience, and trust, is brought to a crashing halt by the corrosive effects of prejudice and favouritism.

In conclusion, the downfall of a commander due to moral failings serves as a powerful reminder of the importance of integrity and fairness in leadership. A commander who fails to uphold these principles, whether through hatred, favouritism, or any other form of bias, jeopardises not only their career but also the well-being and success of their entire unit. Leadership is not a position of power; it is a responsibility to those who follow. When a commander neglects this responsibility, the consequences are far-reaching, and the cost is often paid in the form of lost lives, shattered careers, and a damaged military institution. In the end, the *fall of a 4-star General* is one whose leadership was defined not by their victories, but by the moral compromises that led to their downfall.

*

CHAPTER 7

THE GOOD GENERAL: BUILDING TRUST AND TEAMWORK

A leader's effectiveness in any military organisation is measured not only by their strategic acumen or tactical brilliance but also by their ability to inspire trust, foster loyalty, and build a sense of camaraderie among their troops. Trust and teamwork are the foundation upon which military success is built. A cohesive unit, bound together by mutual respect and shared purpose, is more capable of overcoming the harshest challenges, withstanding adversity, and achieving victory in battle.

The good generals understand this principle intimately and dedicate themselves to cultivating an environment where loyalty, trust, and camaraderie thrive. Good generals are more than just commanders; they are servant-leaders. The best military leaders understand that their role is not to command from a distant ivory tower but to be present and engaged with their troops. They make themselves available, take the time to listen to the concerns and aspirations of those under their command, and lead by example. This approach fosters a sense of trust between the leader and the soldiers, as well as a deep sense of loyalty to the leader and the mission.

Trust is not something that can be demanded; it must be earned. A general who prioritises soldiers' welfare, acknowledges their sacrifices, and shows genuine care for their well-being inspires a level of trust that is essential for operational effectiveness. Soldiers who trust their commander will follow them without hesitation, even in the most dangerous and uncertain circumstances. Trust, once established, creates a bond that allows for open communication, swift decision-making, and a collective sense of purpose that strengthens the unit as a whole.

Loyalty is another cornerstone of a well-functioning military unit. Loyalty in the military context is a two-way street. It is not only the soldiers' loyalty to their commander, but also the commander's loyalty to their troops. The good general understands that loyalty cannot be demanded; it must be earned by showing unwavering support to those under their command.

Loyalty is built over time through consistent actions that demonstrate a commitment to the welfare of the soldiers. A good general takes the time to learn about their soldiers as individuals, listens to their concerns, and ensures that their needs, both professional and personal, are addressed. This mutual loyalty builds a sense of camaraderie, where soldiers feel like they are part of a close-knit team working toward a shared goal.

Camaraderie, the deep bond that develops among soldiers who fight alongside one another, is also a product of effective leadership. The good general understands that military service is not just about training, tactics, and missions. It is also about the relationships that form between soldiers in the trenches. The best leaders actively work to foster a sense of teamwork and brotherhood among their troops. They understand that the strength of a unit lies in the strength of its interpersonal connections. Soldiers who feel a sense of solidarity are more willing to put themselves in harm's way for one another.

This selflessness can make all the difference in high-stress, high-stakes situations.

Case Studies

General George C. Marshall: *A beacon of trust and loyalty*

One of the most iconic examples of a general who inspired loyalty, trust, and camaraderie is General George C. Marshall, who served as Chief of Staff of the United States Army during World War II. Marshall was not just a brilliant strategist; he was a general who deeply cared for his troops and always put their welfare first. His leadership style was characterised by humility, integrity, and an unwavering commitment to his soldiers. He spent time with his troops, listened to their concerns, and ensured they had the resources they needed to succeed.

Marshall's care for his soldiers was evident in his efforts to improve conditions for them during the war. He championed the establishment of better training programmes, improved medical care, and greater attention to the well-being of soldiers on the front lines. Marshall also advocated for the creation of the U.S. Army's first full-time chaplain service, recognising the spiritual and emotional needs of his troops. His deep sense of responsibility for his soldiers' welfare earned him their unwavering loyalty and trust, and his leadership was instrumental in the success of the Allied war effort.

General Dwight D. Eisenhower: *Leading with empathy and teamwork*

Another exemplary leader who prioritised the welfare of his troops was General Dwight D. Eisenhower, Supreme Commander of the Allied Expeditionary Force during World War II. Eisenhower was known for his ability to build and maintain strong, cohesive teams, even in the face of immense challenges.

He demonstrated empathy toward his soldiers, understanding their fears, their struggles, and the hardships they endured. Eisenhower made sure to communicate directly with his soldiers, often visiting front-line units to boost morale and show his support. Eisenhower's leadership style was based on collaboration, inclusivity, and a sense of shared purpose. He understood that victory in war depended not just on individual brilliance but on the collective strength of the team. Eisenhower was able to bring together soldiers from various Allied nations, each with their own cultural and operational differences, and unite them under a common cause. His ability to inspire trust and foster teamwork across diverse groups is one of the key reasons why the Allies were able to achieve victory in Europe. Eisenhower's success in leading large, diverse teams stands as a testament to the power of empathy, communication, and mutual respect in leadership.

General Colin Powell: *Leading with integrity and compassion*

General Colin Powell, former Chairman of the Joint Chiefs of Staff, is another prime example of a leader who built trust and camaraderie within his units. Powell was known for his open, honest communication style and his deep respect for the men and women under his command. He emphasised the importance of developing relationships based on mutual trust and respect. Powell was committed to the welfare of his troops and worked to ensure they had the resources, training, and support they needed to succeed in the demanding environments they faced. Powell's leadership was also marked by his willingness to take responsibility for his decisions, especially in difficult situations. He was known for taking ownership of both successes and failures, earning the respect of those around him.

His leadership inspired loyalty, as his troops trusted that he would always act in their best interest, even in the face of challenges. Powell's leadership style, characterised by empathy, accountability, and integrity, has made him one of the most respected military leaders in modern history.

Trust is the invisible glue that binds a military unit together, and teamwork is the engine that drives its success. In any army, no matter how well-resourced or highly trained, a unit that lacks cohesion and mutual respect is one that risks failure in both peace and war. At the centre of this dynamic is leadership, specifically, the ability of a commander to build a climate where soldiers believe in one another, communicate openly, and operate as a unified force.

Building trust and teamwork is not a checklist to complete, nor a speech to deliver once; it is a continuous, deliberate commitment that must be renewed daily. The best commanders understand that trust is earned, not demanded, and that morale is shaped not only by battlefield victories but by the integrity, humility, and consistency of those in command. In units led by strong and ethical generals, a culture of transparency, mutual support, and shared purpose naturally flourishes. Soldiers know their worth, understand their mission, and feel safe to speak the truth without fear of retaliation. Such environments do not emerge by chance; they are cultivated through intentional leadership practices that prioritise people over position and service over self. The following are key best practices that have consistently proven effective in building trust, loyalty, and comradeship within a military team:

Lead by example

The most effective way to build trust is by setting a positive example. The generals who expect discipline, integrity, and respect from their soldiers must first demonstrate these qualities themselves.

THE VERY VERY BEST BAD 4-STAR GENERAL

Leading by example means living up to the same standards you expect from others. A commander who is honest, dependable, and accountable will inspire the same behaviour in their troops. By consistently modelling the values and behaviours they expect from others, good leaders earn the respect and trust of their soldiers.

Communicate transparently and effectively

Open and honest communication is essential for building trust. Soldiers need to feel that they are informed about decisions that affect them and that their concerns and feedback are valued. A good general maintains open lines of communication with their troops, provides them with the information they need to perform their tasks effectively, and listens to their concerns. Transparency in decision-making fosters trust and helps to eliminate uncertainty, which can lead to confusion or frustration among soldiers.

Invest in the well-being of soldiers

The welfare of soldiers should always be a priority.
A good general recognises that soldiers are human beings with personal lives, emotional needs, and physical well-being that must be addressed in addition to their professional duties. This is done by showing genuine concern for the well-being of their troops. Whether through ensuring proper rest, providing adequate medical care, or offering mental health support, a commander fosters a culture of loyalty and trust. Soldiers who feel valued and cared for are more likely to give their best in service to their commander and their comrades.

Foster a culture of teamwork

A successful military unit operates as a team, not as a collection of individuals. A good general emphasises the importance of teamwork at every level of the organisation.

This can be achieved through joint training exercises, team-building activities, and encouraging collaboration between soldiers of different backgrounds and skill sets. The good general makes it clear that success depends on the collective effort of the unit, not on individual achievements. By fostering a sense of camaraderie and mutual respect, a general creates an environment where soldiers work together toward a common goal, and the strength of the team becomes the key to success.

Recognise and reward excellence

Recognition is a powerful tool to motivate soldiers and build trust. A good general takes the time to recognise the hard work and achievements of their soldiers. Whether through formal awards, promotions, or informal praise, recognition helps soldiers feel valued and reinforces the behaviours that contribute to the success of the unit. By rewarding excellence and acknowledging contributions, the general fosters a culture of accountability, pride, and mutual respect.

Empower soldiers to take initiative

Trust is also built by empowering soldiers to take ownership of their roles and responsibilities. A good general encourages their troops to make decisions and take initiative, knowing that their soldiers will act in the best interest of the unit.
By giving soldiers autonomy to solve problems and contribute to decision-making, the general demonstrates confidence in their abilities and builds a sense of ownership and responsibility within the team.

In conclusion, building trust and teamwork is an essential aspect of military leadership. The best generals are those who prioritise these qualities above all else. By leading with integrity, communicating effectively, and investing in the well-being of their soldiers, commanders can inspire loyalty, foster camaraderie, and create cohesive, high-performing teams. The case studies illustrate how leadership grounded in trust and empathy can have profound and lasting effects on military success. Ultimately, the ability to build trust and teamwork separates the best generals from the rest, ensuring that their units are prepared to face the challenges of war with unity, strength, and resilience.

*

CHAPTER 8

A UNIFIED ARMY: THE STRENGTH OF COLLABORATION

In the vessel of warfare, where chaos, fear, and uncertainty are constant, the true strength of a military force is revealed. While superior firepower and tactical brilliance play their roles, history has shown time and again that it is unity which tips the balance between victory and defeat. A fragmented army is vulnerable no matter how well-equipped it is. A unified force, bound by trust, guided by purpose, and driven by a spirit of collaboration, becomes an unbreakable front against any enemy.

Collaboration is not a luxury in military operations; it is a necessity. It bridges the gap between ranks, departments, and individual roles, transforming a collection of soldiers into a cohesive, battle-ready machine. It turns communication into clarity, diversity into strength, and challenges into shared opportunities. The most successful military campaigns in history have been won not by lone heroes, but by teams that moved, fought, and believed as one. This chapter delves into the often-overlooked yet critical element of internal military collaboration.

We examine how commanders can cultivate environments where cooperation thrives, how mutual respect can replace rivalry, and how a shared vision, rooted in duty and patriotism, can forge an unstoppable army. For in unity lies the heart of victory.

Collaboration in the military, at its core, is a product of a shared vision and mutual respect between all members of the force. A shared vision is not merely a set of goals or objectives. It is a deep, collective understanding of what the military is trying to achieve. It is a purpose that drives every soldier and officer, and a sense of ownership that everyone has in the success of the mission. The most effective military leaders understand that their responsibility is not only to devise strategy and issue orders, but also to ensure that every member of their force shares a broader vision of the organisation.

When a military is united by a shared vision, there is a collective commitment to the cause. Each soldier, from the highest-ranking officer to the lowest-ranking private, understands their role within the larger mission and recognises the importance of their contributions to the success of the whole. This unity of purpose is what binds soldiers to their leaders and to each other. It transforms what might otherwise be a disparate group of individuals into a cohesive team, all working toward the same objective. In this environment, collaboration becomes natural because every member of the military knows that their efforts are part of something greater than themselves.

Mutual respect is the other key ingredient that fuels collaboration. Respect in the military is not a given; it must be earned through consistent actions, fair treatment, and the demonstration of competence. A leader who commands respect is one who inspires confidence, fairness, and admiration in their subordinates.

Respect is reciprocated when officers trust their soldiers and when soldiers have confidence in their officers. This respect creates an environment in which all individuals, regardless of rank, feel valued and empowered to contribute their ideas, expertise, and efforts. When soldiers know that their voices matter, they are more likely to collaborate freely and openly, leading to better outcomes for the entire unit.

Respect and shared vision, therefore, are intertwined. They create an atmosphere in which collaboration is not a forced or artificial process but rather an organic and inherent part of the military's culture. Leaders who prioritise respect and clarity in their vision lay the groundwork for a unified force that is both effective and resilient in the face of challenges.

The most successful military campaigns in history have often been defined by the strength of collaboration between officers and soldiers. While officers are tasked with making strategic decisions, developing plans, and commanding the battlefield, the soldiers are the ones who execute these decisions and bring those plans to life. A cohesive working relationship between officers and soldiers is essential for turning abstract strategies into concrete actions. This collaboration ensures that the military operates as a unified mechanism, with all parties working in harmony toward the same goal.

Officers play a critical role in creating the conditions necessary for effective collaboration. It is the officer's responsibility to clearly articulate the vision and mission and to ensure that every member of the force understands not only what needs to be done but why it is important. A good officer communicates this vision in such a way that soldiers can see their role within the larger framework of the military's objectives. This clarity enables soldiers to make decisions on the ground that align with the overall strategy.

However, effective officers also understand that collaboration is not about top-down command and control; it is about empowering soldiers to use their initiative and expertise in pursuit of the mission. Officers who foster collaboration do not micromanage but instead trust their soldiers to make decisions that contribute to the success of the operation. This level of autonomy enhances the soldiers' sense of ownership, responsibility, and accountability, which in turn strengthens their commitment to the mission and to each other. By creating a culture in which soldiers feel empowered and valued, officers can tap into the collective knowledge and capabilities of the entire unit. This collective intelligence, when harnessed through collaboration, often results in innovative solutions, greater adaptability, and improved decision-making on the battlefield.

It is imperative to note that while officers are responsible for leading and directing the force, soldiers are the ones who execute the plans and bring them to fruition. For collaboration to be effective, soldiers must be well-trained, well-equipped, and, most importantly, motivated. Soldiers who feel respected, trusted, and valued by their officers are more likely to invest themselves fully in their tasks and contribute to the success of the mission. Collaboration between soldiers and officers is strengthened when soldiers feel that their ideas and feedback are taken seriously. In environments where soldiers' contributions are encouraged and acted upon, soldiers feel a sense of ownership and pride in their work. This not only improves morale but also strengthens the unit's overall effectiveness. In the heat of battle, the bond between officers and soldiers built on mutual respect and shared purpose can make all the difference. Soldiers who trust their officers to make sound decisions will fight harder, take risks when necessary, and work as a cohesive unit to achieve victory.

Case Studies

Throughout military history, numerous examples illustrate the power of collaboration in achieving victory. These case studies highlight the symbiotic relationship between officers and soldiers, demonstrating how their cooperation leads to military success.

The Battle of Waterloo (1815)

One of the most famous examples of collaboration between officers and soldiers occurred during the Battle of Waterloo. The Allied forces, led by the Duke of Wellington, faced Napoleon Bonaparte's army in a decisive confrontation. Wellington's leadership style was characterised by his ability to foster strong relationships with his officers and soldiers. He was known for spending time with his troops, ensuring they understood the battle plan and their individual roles within it. His officers, in turn, communicated the plan effectively to the soldiers, ensuring everyone was aligned in their objectives. This mutual respect and collaboration between the Duke and his forces, from officers down to the rank and file, was key to their ability to withstand the brutal onslaught of Napoleon's forces. The battle was won not by superior tactics or technology but by the unrelenting collaboration between officers and soldiers, each trusting in the others' abilities and commitment.

The Normandy Invasion (D-Day, 1944)

Another exemplary case of collaboration occurred during the D-Day landings in World War II. General Dwight D. Eisenhower and his officers worked tirelessly to devise the invasion plan, but it was the soldiers who carried out the operation under the most difficult and dangerous conditions. The success of the invasion hinged on the ability of officers to coordinate across multiple nations and branches of the military while ensuring that soldiers on the ground had the flexibility to make real-time decisions as they encountered unforeseen challenges. Eisenhower's emphasis on clear communication, mutual respect, and shared responsibility among his officers and soldiers helped ensure that the operation was a success. The soldiers, aware of the enormity of the mission, fought with unyielding determination, trusting their officers to guide them. This collaboration across all ranks played a pivotal role in the success of the invasion and the eventual defeat of Nazi forces.

In modern warfare, collaboration has become even more crucial. The complexity of contemporary military operations, which often involve multiple branches of the armed forces, allied nations, and specialised units, requires seamless cooperation and coordination at all levels. Officers must ensure that their soldiers are equipped with the best technology, intelligence, and training, while soldiers trust in the leadership of their officers to navigate the ever-evolving challenges of the battlefield. Advances in technology, such as communications systems, surveillance tools, and real-time data sharing, have enabled greater collaboration between units. The ability to share information quickly and accurately across the battlefield has made collaboration even more important. In modern conflicts, soldiers and officers alike must be able to adapt to rapidly changing situations, and the strength of their collaboration is what allows them to do so effectively.

In conclusion, the strength of any military force lies not just in its weapons, tactics, or resources. It lies in the unity of purpose and collaboration between its officers and soldiers. A unified army, driven by a shared vision and mutual respect, is a force that can overcome even the most formidable challenges.

Through effective collaboration, officers and soldiers form a cohesive unit that can adapt to the complexities of warfare, make timely and accurate decisions, and execute strategies with precision.

As demonstrated by historical case studies and modern warfare practices, collaboration is the cornerstone of military success. When officers and soldiers work together, fully understand their roles, responsibilities, and shared objectives, they form an unbreakable bond that can win wars and achieve victory on the battlefield.

*

CHAPTER 9

WHEN SOLDIERS SUFFER: THE CONSEQUENCES OF BAD LEADERSHIP

Leadership in the military is a weighty responsibility that carries with it the duty to safeguard not just the physical well-being of soldiers but also their psychological and emotional welfare. The price of bad leadership can be steep, resulting in lasting effects that extend far beyond the battlefield. Soldiers who are under poor leadership may endure physical harm, but it is often the psychological and emotional toll that leaves scars that do not easily heal. Bad leadership can create an environment where morale is crushed, trust is shattered, and the bonds of camaraderie that are essential to military success are irreparably damaged. In this chapter, we examine the consequences of bad leadership, from the suffering it inflicts on soldiers to the broader impact it has on the effectiveness and cohesion of the military. Through historical examples, we explore how poor leadership can lead to defeat, desertion, and even the loss of life.

Bad leadership is often a catalyst for suffering among soldiers, as it manifests in several ways, psychologically, emotionally, and physically. The most immediate and obvious consequence of poor leadership is the erosion of morale.

THE VERY VERY BEST BAD 4-STAR GENERAL

When soldiers are led by incompetent or cruel commanders, their motivation to perform their duties diminishes, and their sense of purpose is undermined. Without strong leadership, soldiers begin to feel that their efforts are futile and that their lives are at risk for causes that are either unclear or unworthy. This loss of morale leads to disengagement, lower performance, and sometimes even insubordination, all of which compromise the effectiveness of the unit.

On the psychological front, bad leadership can have profound and lasting effects on soldiers' mental health. When soldiers are exposed to leaders who are negligent, abusive, or incapable, they experience stress, anxiety, and a sense of powerlessness. Poor leadership can lead to a breakdown in communication, where soldiers feel unable to voice concerns or seek guidance. In extreme cases, soldiers who are subjected to bad leadership may develop symptoms of Post-Traumatic Stress Disorder (PTSD), depression, or other mental health issues. The constant uncertainty and fear that come from having an unstable or unpredictable leader can exacerbate these conditions, leading to long-term psychological damage that may affect soldiers long after their service has ended.

Emotionally, soldiers rely on their leaders for guidance, support, and reassurance, especially during times of adversity. A good leader fosters an environment of trust and comradeship that ensures that soldiers feel valued and understood. In contrast, bad leadership breeds fear, distrust, and division. Soldiers may feel abandoned or betrayed when their leaders fail to show empathy, act with integrity, or prioritise the welfare of the unit over personal gain. Emotional trauma can also result from the leader's failure to properly handle situations of conflict, creating an atmosphere of tension and hostility within the ranks. The emotional toll of bad leadership can tear apart unit cohesion, leaving soldiers isolated and disconnected from each other.

Physically, the toll of poor leadership can manifest in more direct ways. Incompetent leadership often results in poorly executed plans and strategies, which can lead to unnecessary casualties, injuries, and loss of life. A leader who fails to provide clear guidance or who makes reckless decisions places soldiers in harm's way unnecessarily. Inadequate preparation, lack of proper equipment, and poor logistical support, often the consequences of bad leadership, can put soldiers at risk during combat. Furthermore, leaders who fail to recognise the physical needs of their troops, such as ensuring proper rest, nutrition, and medical care, can exacerbate fatigue and sickness, ultimately compromising the soldiers' ability to perform their duties effectively.

Historical examples

Throughout history, there have been numerous examples where bad leadership led to disastrous consequences for soldiers, causing defeat, desertion, and, in some cases, the loss of thousands of lives. These examples serve as stark reminders of the importance of competent, responsible leadership in the military.

The Charge of the Light Brigade (1854)

One of the most infamous examples of bad leadership resulting in unnecessary loss of life occurred during the Crimean War, the Charge of the Light Brigade. The British cavalry, under the command of Lord Cardigan, was ordered to charge Russian artillery positions at the Battle of Balaclava. However, due to a miscommunication between commanders, the order was misunderstood, and the Light Brigade charged directly into the face of a heavily fortified Russian artillery battery. The result was a slaughter, with over 600 men killed or wounded.

THE VERY VERY BEST BAD 4-STAR GENERAL

This incident was a direct result of poor leadership at multiple levels. Lord Cardigan's failure to question the order or to seek clarification when the command was unclear led to the soldiers being sent to their deaths. Additionally, the lack of coordination between higher-ranking officers and the failure to properly assess the risks and consequences of the order demonstrated a complete disregard for the welfare of the soldiers under their command. The psychological and emotional toll of this disaster was immense, not only on the soldiers who fought but also on their families and the British public, who struggled to understand how such a tragedy could have been allowed to happen.

The Battle of Stalingrad (1942-1943)

The Battle of Stalingrad during World War II is another example of how poor leadership can lead to devastating consequences. The battle, one of the bloodiest in history, was characterised by the German army's brutal and relentless push into the Soviet Union. Under the command of General Friedrich Paulus, the German Sixth Army became bogged down in a prolonged siege, facing harsh winter conditions, inadequate supplies, and an unrelenting Soviet counteroffensive.

The leadership failures of General Paulus and his commanders were critical in the defeat of the German forces. Paulus made several miscalculations, including underestimating the Soviet resolve and the logistical challenges of maintaining an extended siege. He was also unable to effectively coordinate with other German forces, leaving his troops vulnerable to encirclement. The suffering endured by the German soldiers was immense, with thousands dying from cold, starvation, and wounds, while many others were taken prisoner. The defeat at Stalingrad was a turning point in the war, demonstrating the disastrous impact of poor leadership on both the physical and psychological well-being of soldiers.

On the Soviet side, the leadership of General Vasily Chuikov, though not without its own flaws, was characterised by a tenacious defence and a deep understanding of the strategic importance of Stalingrad. While Soviet soldiers faced extreme hardships, they were motivated by strong leadership, clear objectives, and a sense of national purpose, which helped them endure the suffering and eventually emerge victorious.

The Vietnam War (1955-1975)

The Vietnam War offers another poignant example of how bad leadership can lead to both military defeat and societal damage. The war was marked by a series of poor strategic decisions, mismanagement, and leadership failures, particularly by senior U.S. commanders. A lack of clear objectives, coupled with an inadequate understanding of the political and cultural dynamics of Vietnam, resulted in a conflict that dragged on for years without significant progress.

One of the most glaring examples of leadership failure occurred during the Tet Offensive of 1968. United States military commanders, underestimating the resolve of the North Vietnamese forces, failed to anticipate the magnitude of the attack, leading to a surprise offensive that resulted in significant casualties. The psychological toll on American soldiers was profound, as many began to lose confidence in their leadership and the prospects for victory. Desertion rates increased, and morale plummeted, as soldiers faced a leadership that seemed out of touch with the realities of the war.

The leadership failures in Vietnam had long-lasting effects on the soldiers who fought there. Many veterans returned home traumatised, grappling with issues such as PTSD, substance abuse, and a profound sense of disillusionment.

The emotional scars of bad leadership during the war affected generations of soldiers and their families, underscoring the importance of competent, compassionate leadership in times of conflict.

The Rwandan Genocide (1994)

In more recent history, the leadership failures that led to the Rwandan Genocide highlight the devastating consequences of bad military and political leadership. In the months leading up to the genocide, the Rwandan army, under the command of General Augustin Bizimungu, was complicit in inciting and carrying out acts of violence against the Tutsi population.

The soldiers, many of whom were poorly trained and indoctrinated by propaganda, were directed to carry out atrocities that led to the deaths of an estimated 800,000 people. The failure of leadership, both in the military and government, was profound. Bad leaders exploited ethnic divisions and manipulated soldiers to carry out horrific acts of violence.

The emotional and psychological toll on the soldiers involved in the genocide was immense. Many were coerced or brainwashed into committing atrocities, and the aftermath of their involvement left many with deep psychological scars. The long-term effects of this bad leadership continue to affect the survivors of the genocide, as well as the soldiers who were involved.

In conclusion, bad leadership in the military is a powerful force that can bring untold suffering to soldiers and irreparable harm to the effectiveness of the military. The psychological, emotional, and physical toll that poor leadership inflicts on soldiers is profound, as it leaves scars that may never fully heal.

THE VERY VERY BEST BAD 4-STAR GENERAL

The historical examples of bad leadership demonstrate how incompetence, negligence, and miscommunication can lead to unnecessary suffering, defeat, desertion, and loss of life. Leadership is not just about making decisions; it is about understanding the human cost of those decisions and being accountable for the welfare of those who are entrusted to your care. In military operations, where the stakes are often life and death, the consequences of bad leadership can be catastrophic, often leaving lasting effects on soldiers and their families, as well as on the overall success or failure of military campaigns.

*

CHAPTER 10

LEADERSHIP IN PEACETIME: THE IMPORTANCE OF PREPARATION

In the grand needlepoint of military leadership, the importance of peacetime is often underestimated. Many may think that leadership is only crucial during times of war, when the stakes are high and the pressure is intense. However, it is during peacetime that the foundations for future success or failure are laid. Effective military leaders understand the significance of peacetime. They use this time to not only prepare for future conflicts but to build a robust and adaptive army capable of responding to any challenge that may arise. Leadership in peacetime requires foresight, discipline, and vision. Strong leaders use peacetime to develop strategy, cultivate talent, and prepare their troops for the rigours of war.

Conversely, bad Generals who neglect these responsibilities risk the very survival of their military forces. This usually leads to strategic failures, disjointed operations, and a lack of readiness when the call to battle eventually comes. Peacetime is often perceived as a period of tranquillity, an interlude between conflicts. For military leaders, however, it is far from a time of rest. It is a time of preparation, reflection, and strategic foresight.

Strong leadership during peacetime is not about resting on successes or assuming that the forces will be ready when the need arises. Instead, it is about shaping an army that is resilient, adaptive, and capable of responding swiftly and effectively to the unpredictable nature of warfare. The primary role of leadership in peacetime is to ensure that the military remains combat-ready, both mentally and physically. During peacetime, military leaders are responsible for planning and strategising for future conflicts. This is to ensure that their forces are prepared for a wide range of scenarios. This involves understanding the current geopolitical climate, analysing potential threats, and developing strategies to counter those threats. Leaders use this time to refine their forces' operational readiness, strengthen their capabilities, and ensure that every soldier is trained, equipped, and prepared for the harsh realities of war.

Furthermore, peacetime provides an opportunity for military leaders to focus on the well-being of their troops. Strong leaders recognise that the health and morale of their soldiers are just as critical to success as tactical prowess.

Leadership in peacetime involves fostering a positive culture within the military, one where soldiers are encouraged to develop professionally, maintain physical fitness, and build strong, cohesive teams. These efforts lay the groundwork for resilience in times of crisis.

A critical responsibility of leadership during peacetime is the development of a strategy. Strategy is the art of war that transcends the battlefield. It shapes the direction of military forces, determining the resources allocated to different objectives and setting the tone for future conflicts. Effective Generals use peacetime to craft long-term strategies, considering both current realities and future contingencies.

Strategic planning during peacetime requires a deep understanding of national security goals, potential threats, and the capabilities of both friendly and adversarial forces.

It involves analysing the lessons learnt from past conflicts and anticipating the demands of future warfare. The best Generals take a holistic approach to strategy. They consider not only military objectives but also the political, social, and economic dimensions that influence military success. They engage in continuous assessment and recalibration of their strategy to ensure that it remains relevant and adaptable to changing circumstances.

In practical terms, this means identifying areas where military capabilities need to be strengthened. This is whether through the development of new technologies, the enhancement of training programmes, or the strategic positioning of forces. It also means considering the future roles of the military. This includes how the army, navy, air force, and Special Forces will be integrated into a unified strategy that can address multiple threats. The strategic decisions made during peacetime set the conditions for future conflict, and a failure to prepare can lead to disastrous outcomes when conflict inevitably arises.

Another crucial element of leadership during peacetime is the cultivation of talent. An army is only as strong as the people who serve in it. Strong leaders recognise the importance of developing the next generation of military leaders. Peacetime provides the ideal opportunity for training, mentorship, and leadership development. This ensures that the soldiers of today are prepared to lead the soldiers of tomorrow. Leaders in peacetime must invest in the professional development of their troops. This involves providing training that goes beyond basic military skills. It includes the development of critical thinking, problem-solving, and leadership capabilities.

By offering advanced training programmes, military education, and exposure to diverse experiences, leaders can prepare their subordinates for the challenges they will face in future conflicts. The goal is to create a culture of continuous learning where every soldier, from the lowest-ranking private to the highest-ranking officer, is encouraged to develop and improve their skills.

In addition to formal training programmes, effective leaders foster mentorship relationships that allow senior officers to impart their knowledge and wisdom to junior officers. Mentorship ensures that leadership styles, values, and traditions are passed down through generations, creating a cohesive and effective military culture. Strong leaders also recognise the importance of diversity in leadership, encouraging soldiers from different backgrounds to rise through the ranks and contribute their unique perspectives to the organisation. This not only strengthens the military's ability to adapt to different challenges but also cultivates a sense of inclusivity and unity within the ranks.

One of the most important tasks of leadership during peacetime is to prepare troops for the mental, emotional, and physical rigours of war. This is not just about teaching soldiers how to operate weapons or follow orders. It is about preparing them for the brutal reality of combat: the stress, the fear, and the emotional toll it takes. Peacetime allows leaders to focus on mental resilience and ensuring that soldiers are mentally prepared for the challenges they will face on the battlefield.

Training exercises during peacetime should simulate as much of the chaos and unpredictability of war as possible. This includes joint exercises with allied forces, training in unfamiliar terrain, and exposure to different combat scenarios.

These simulations allow soldiers to learn how to respond quickly and effectively under pressure, making decisions in real-time and maintaining their composure in the heat of battle. It is also important for leaders to instil a sense of teamwork and solidarity during these training periods. The bonds formed between soldiers during peacetime can prove invaluable in times of war, when trust and unity are critical for success. Moreover, preparing troops for war requires addressing the psychological aspects of combat. Effective leaders ensure that soldiers receive proper mental health support, including stress management programmes, counselling, and debriefing after missions. This proactive approach to mental health helps prevent the long-term emotional scars that can result from prolonged exposure to combat.

While strong leadership during peacetime can lay the foundation for success in war, bad leadership that neglects preparation can have disastrous consequences. Generals who fail to plan risk the readiness of their forces, leaving them vulnerable to unforeseen threats. Neglecting strategic development, talent cultivation, and mental preparation can lead to poor performance in battle, unnecessary casualties, and even defeat.

One of the most significant consequences of bad leadership during peacetime is the erosion of trust within the military. If leaders fail to engage with their troops, invest in their training, or provide the resources necessary for readiness, soldiers may begin to question the leaders' competence and commitment to their welfare. This loss of confidence can have a profound impact on morale, making it difficult for soldiers to follow orders or work together effectively in combat. Without a strong foundation of trust, even the most capable military force will struggle to function cohesively in times of crisis.

Another consequence of neglecting preparation is the inability to adapt to new and evolving threats. Modern warfare is rapidly changing, with technological advancements and shifting geopolitical dynamics creating new challenges for military forces. Generals who do not recognise the need for continuous adaptation and development risk finding themselves unprepared for these challenges. Whether it is cyber warfare, asymmetric conflicts, or new weapons systems, failure to stay ahead of these developments can lead to strategic disadvantages and defeat.

Bad leadership during peacetime can result in a failure to properly equip and train troops. This can lead to inadequately prepared soldiers who are ill-equipped to handle the realities of war. The consequences are not just tactical. Poor preparation can result in the unnecessary loss of life, both of soldiers and civilians. It can lead to broader strategic failures that have long-lasting repercussions for national security.

Conclusively, leadership in peacetime is not a luxury; it is a necessity. Strong military leaders understand that peacetime is the foundation upon which the success of future operations rests. They use this time wisely, developing strategy, cultivating talent, and preparing their troops for the challenges ahead. Peacetime is an opportunity to shape the future of the military, to ensure that it is adaptable, resilient, and ready to respond to any threat. Leaders who neglect this responsibility risk leaving their forces unprepared and setting the stage for failure when the inevitable call to war comes. The contrast between strong and weak leadership during peacetime could not be clearer. The former creates armies capable of achieving victory, while the latter sows the seeds of defeat. Therefore, military leadership in peacetime is not just about maintaining the status quo but about actively shaping a future where the military is prepared, unified, and capable of overcoming any challenge.

CHAPTER 11

THE LEADERSHIP VACUUM: WHEN GOOD LEADERS ARE GONE

Leadership in any organisation, especially within a military context, is integral to its functionality, morale, and operational effectiveness. In the world of armed forces, leaders not only direct strategic operations but also shape the culture and ethos of the institution they oversee. Strong leadership can inspire loyalty, cohesion, and unwavering dedication. The absence of competent leadership can lead to disarray, confusion, and, in some cases, outright chaos. When a respected leader exits the scene suddenly, be it due to death, resignation, or other unforeseen circumstances, it results in a leadership vacuum that can be devastating. The absence of strong, guiding figures in the ranks is a crisis that demands immediate and efficient resolution. However, the reality of such a vacuum is often far more complicated. It can be exacerbated by weak, corrupt, or self-serving individuals who seek to exploit the situation for their personal gain.

This chapter will explore the detrimental effects of losing a great leader and the cascading consequences for the military. We will delve into the challenges of transitioning to new leadership, the dangers posed by weak or unscrupulous successors, and historical examples of organisations that struggled during these pivotal moments. Through case studies and examples, we will highlight the necessity of robust succession planning, mentorship, and strategic foresight to avoid the chaos that often follows the sudden departure of a strong leader.

The absence of a strong leader creates a void that, if not addressed quickly, can spiral into dysfunction within the ranks. Leaders are not just figureheads; they are the linchpins that hold military organisations together. They set the tone, create a vision, and, importantly, provide direction during moments of crisis. Without this central figure, soldiers, officers, and command structures can quickly find themselves uncertain and unable to move forward with purpose. The organisational fabric weakens, and morale can take a dramatic hit.

When a beloved and respected leader dies, resigns, or is otherwise removed, there is an emotional impact that echoes throughout the ranks. The sense of loss is not merely personal but institutional. The leader's vision, strategic insight, and leadership style often infiltrate the daily operations of the military. Soldiers, officers, and support personnel alike may feel directionless, unsure of how to proceed without their trusted guide. The loss may also lead to anxiety about the future direction of the military, as people worry whether their new leader will uphold the legacy or values that were established under the previous regime. In these instances, the military is vulnerable to fragmentation, as factions may begin to form, some aligned with the old regime and others with the new leadership.

The immediate aftermath can also bring about confusion in decision-making. Leaders who served under the departing General may be unsure whether they should continue executing prior orders or wait for the new leadership to issue new directives. Without clear communication and quick resolution, this uncertainty can lead to operational stagnation and missed opportunities.

THE VERY VERY BEST BAD 4-STAR GENERAL

While the loss of a leader creates an immediate leadership vacuum, the real danger lies in who fills the void. In an ideal world, there would always be a capable, trained successor ready to step into the role to ensure a smooth transition. However, this is not always the case. Weak or corrupt successors can quickly capitalise on a leadership vacuum, undermining the effectiveness and integrity of the entire military apparatus.

A weak leader, one who lacks the requisite skills, vision, or character to lead, can cause irreparable damage to the organisation. These leaders often lack the respect of their subordinates. They are unable to make decisive, informed decisions, and this leads to hesitation and disarray. A leader who fails to inspire confidence will struggle to maintain control. This creates internal divisions and fosters a climate of mistrust. Troops may begin to question their new leader's ability to guide them, and this undermines morale and cohesion. With low morale comes a decline in discipline, performance, and overall effectiveness, vital elements for a military to function properly, especially in times of conflict or crisis.

Corrupt leadership is arguably even more dangerous. When leaders see the vacuum as an opportunity to enrich themselves or assert personal power, they risk not only weakening the military but also jeopardising its integrity and purpose. Corruption can manifest in many forms: bribery, manipulation, abuse of power, or even the prioritisation of personal or political interests over the good of the military or nation. Such leaders often surround themselves with individuals who are loyal to them for selfish reasons, rather than based on merit or professionalism. This toxic environment breeds dishonesty, incompetence, and cronyism, further eroding the military's operational capabilities and overall trust within the ranks.

THE VERY VERY BEST BAD 4-STAR GENERAL

Corruption in a time of leadership transition is a particularly insidious problem. A leader who consolidates power through unethical means may exploit the lack of oversight to secure their own position while compromising the military's readiness and effectiveness. The damage can be long-lasting. Corrupt leaders often abandon or neglect critical tasks, including resource allocation, troop welfare, and strategy development, focusing instead on securing their personal hold on power.

Even when a new leader is both capable and well-intentioned, the process of transitioning from one leader to another is fraught with challenges. Military organisations, especially large and complex ones, are not designed to function without clear leadership. The shift from one leader to another requires careful planning, coordination, and communication. Without these elements, the military risks descending into chaos.

One of the primary challenges during a leadership transition is maintaining operational continuity. The new leader must quickly establish authority while respecting the decisions made by their predecessor. They must ensure that there is no gap in operational activity, which means stepping into the role without delay. However, this can be difficult, as the new leader may face opposition from those loyal to the former leader or from factions within the ranks who have their own ambitions or grievances. The incoming leader must balance the need for immediate action with the importance of fostering unity and consensus.

Moreover, transitioning leadership is a process that requires effective communication. A successful leader must articulate their vision and strategy clearly to the rest of the military. The troops must understand what the new leadership stands for and what they can expect in terms of direction and focus. Failure to communicate this effectively can lead to confusion, unrest, and even disobedience.

Another critical element of successful leadership transition is the ability to inspire confidence in the troops. The new leader must earn the trust of the men and women under their command. This is not something that can be done overnight. Building this trust takes time and effort. A leader who is unable to do so quickly may find themselves struggling to gain the respect necessary to lead effectively.

Case Studies

One of the most glaring examples of a leadership vacuum can be seen in the aftermath of the death of General Erwin Rommel, one of Nazi Germany's most respected and skilled commanders during World War II. Rommel's passing created a void in German command that was not adequately filled by his successors. The resulting loss of cohesion and strategic missteps contributed to the eventual collapse of German military effectiveness during the latter part of the war.

Similarly, the fall of the Soviet Union saw a massive leadership vacuum within its military and political structures. Following the death of prominent leaders like Leonid Brezhnev and the instability of the subsequent leadership changes, the Soviet military began to lose its operational efficiency and strategic coherence. A lack of solid succession planning and an over-reliance on centralised power left the military vulnerable to internal corruption, inefficiency, and lack of direction.

On a more recent note, the post-2003 invasion of Iraq revealed the dangers of a leadership vacuum within the Iraqi military. After the fall of Saddam Hussein's regime, Iraq's military was left in disarray, and the absence of strong, capable leadership contributed to the army's failure to counter insurgency forces effectively.

The absence of a clear transition strategy and the dissolution of the army without solid leadership contributed to the rise of groups like the Islamic State of Iraq and Syria (ISIS), which exploited the gaps in Iraq's defence.

A silent crisis in transition

The passing of a revered and disciplined officer, who remained a symbol of loyalty and patriotism even in retirement, marked a significant moment in the defence force. The subsequent retirement of the long-serving Army Commander signalled a major turning point in its leadership history. Both leaders, despite their different roles and periods of influence, represented a standard of military professionalism, ethical command, and unwavering allegiance to the throne. What followed their departure was not just a routine leadership reshuffle but an apparent crisis of continuity and competence. The commanders who succeeded the General inherited the structure but lacked the unifying authority and strategic foresight that defined their predecessor. Observers within and outside the force noticed a disturbing trend, including promotions based on allegiance to personalities rather than merit, the sidelining of competent officers, the rise of fear-driven command cultures, and a general erosion of institutional discipline and morale.

This leadership drift has raised questions not only about the military's preparedness and professionalism but also about its loyalty to national ideals versus individual ambitions. Allegations of politicisation, internal divisions, and the use of traditional beliefs (muti) to hold power reflect a loss of the rational command culture and professionalism that once characterised the defence force under more disciplined leadership. The replacement of long-serving commanders without a structured leadership renewal strategy also created internal tensions, power struggles, and suspicions of purges.

Career soldiers and officers found themselves at the mercy of political manoeuvring and senior command insecurities. The repeated changes in military leadership and appointments amidst civil unrest saw the armed forces overwhelmed by fragmentation, lack of loyalty, and diminished morale. The lack of continuity in military doctrine and the manipulation of military leadership for political and selfish gains ultimately weakened national defence capabilities.

This experience underscores the need for deliberate leadership succession planning, strategic mentorship, and merit-based promotions. Where transitions are driven by fear, favouritism, or superstition, institutional decline becomes inevitable. Therefore, the survival and integrity of any armed force depend not only on its arsenal but also on its ability to maintain continuity of values, competence, and vision across generations of leadership.

One of the key lessons from these case studies is the importance of succession planning and mentorship within the military. Leaders who ensure that their subordinates are adequately prepared to take on leadership roles when the time comes are creating a legacy of preparedness and stability. Succession planning allows for a seamless transition of power, ensuring that the military is never left without a strong leader at its helm. Effective mentorship programmes also help groom the next generation of leaders, ensuring that leadership qualities, knowledge, and skills are passed down, thus safeguarding the military's ability to function even in the event of a sudden leadership vacuum.

For military organisations, a culture of mentorship is essential to bridging the gap between generations of leaders. Senior officers must take the time to impart knowledge, wisdom, and experiences to those below them to ensure that there is always a deep pool of capable leaders ready to step up when needed.

Through mentorship, emerging leaders can learn from the successes and failures of their predecessors, ensuring that they are better prepared to lead when the time comes.

In conclusion, the leadership vacuum that occurs when strong leaders are gone is one of the most dangerous and destabilising events that can occur within any military organisation. The absence of strong leadership creates a crisis that demands swift and careful resolution. Weak, corrupt, or inexperienced leaders can worsen the situation, causing conflict, failed operations, and even the collapse of military effectiveness. By learning from history and prioritising succession, mentorship, and communication, militaries can manage leadership transitions and prevent chaos. Strong leadership is the cornerstone of any effective military, and it is crucial to ensure that the next generation of leaders is prepared to take up the mantle when the time comes.

*

CHAPTER 12

THE SILENT COST OF POOR LEADERSHIP: INSTITUTIONAL EROSION

The impact of poor leadership within a military organisation is often not immediately visible. It manifests in subtle, creeping ways that accumulate over time. This chapter explores the quiet but long-term damage caused by bad leadership, with a focus on institutional erosion. When a military is led by a General who is ineffective, corrupt, or unqualified, the consequences are far-reaching and often go unnoticed until the damage has already taken root.

The erosion of professionalism, the rise of corruption, and the gradual loss of trust within the ranks can lead to a toxic culture that undermines the military's capacity to function at its full potential. Even worse, these issues often have ripple effects that last for generations, impacting not just the current soldiers but those who come after them. The silent costs of poor leadership may be difficult to quantify, but their consequences are profound and lasting, affecting everything from mission readiness to national security. Corruption is one of the most insidious effects of poor leadership. When a General prioritises self-interest or politics over the institution and its soldiers, it fosters an environment for unethical behaviour.

Corruption can take many forms within the military; misallocation of resources, bribery, abuse of power, and favouritism are just a few examples. While these actions may appear harmless in the short term, they have far-reaching consequences that deteriorate the military's foundation. The first and most immediate consequence of corruption is the mismanagement of resources.

A General who is focused on securing personal benefits through corrupt means often diverts funds and supplies. This misallocation of resources can directly impact the readiness of the military. Training programmes may suffer due to a lack of proper funding. Soldiers may go without essential equipment, and logistical operations may be severely hampered. As a result, the military becomes less capable of performing its duties effectively, and mission readiness is compromised.

Furthermore, corruption erodes the trust that is vital for the functioning of the military. When soldiers see their leaders engaging in unethical behaviour, it creates a culture of cynicism and resentment. Soldiers may begin to question the integrity of the entire system, leading to a breakdown in discipline and morale. A culture of corruption creates an environment where loyalty is based on personal connections or bribes rather than merit and professionalism. This undermines the cohesion and unity that are critical in a military organisation, making it harder for units to function as a cohesive whole.

The effects of corruption also extend beyond immediate leadership. As the culture of corruption spreads through the ranks, it becomes normalised. New recruits, who enter the military with ideals of service, discipline, and honour, can quickly be influenced by the toxic behaviour around them. Over time, this leads to a military institution where corruption is deeply embedded, making it difficult to reform and rebuild trust.

In the worst-case scenario, corruption becomes institutionalised, with entire sectors of the military operating with a sense of entitlement, manipulation, and dishonesty. This institutional rot can take decades to undo, if it can be undone at all.

Trust is the bedrock upon which military organisations are built. Without trust in leaders and in each other, soldiers become less committed to their mission and more likely to question orders. Bad Generals undermine this trust by failing to lead with integrity. They make decisions that are self-serving or contradictory and neglect to communicate openly and honestly with their subordinates. When trust in leadership erodes, soldiers may begin to second-guess their orders or, worse, refuse to follow them altogether.

The consequences of a loss of trust are far-reaching. In a combat situation, where split-second decisions can mean the difference between victory and defeat, soldiers who lack trust in their leaders are less likely to execute orders swiftly and decisively. This hesitation can lead to missed opportunities, operational delays, and even failure on the battlefield. Moreover, the loss of trust extends beyond the relationship between leaders and subordinates. It affects the bonds between soldiers, diminishing the comradeship that is necessary for successful teamwork. In a military environment, where lives are often at stake, the absence of trust can be fatal.

Trust is not something that can be regained easily. Once a General has eroded trust within the ranks, it is difficult to rebuild. Trust is built over time through consistent actions that demonstrate competence, fairness, and reliability. A leader who fails to lead with integrity will find it difficult, if not impossible, to restore the faith of their troops. The loss of trust breeds fear and suspicion, making soldiers protect themselves instead of relying on their leaders. This can lead to an environment where soldiers are more focused on their personal survival rather than the collective good of the military.

THE VERY VERY BEST BAD 4-STAR GENERAL

In the long term, a military institution that operates without trust becomes a hollow shell of its former self. Morale drops, and soldiers begin to disengage from their work. Instead of being motivated by a shared sense of duty and purpose, they are simply going through the motions. The result is a military that is ill-prepared to meet future challenges. The loss of trust has consequences that extend beyond the individual soldier; it affects the entire structure, creating a fractured and ineffective organisation.

Professionalism is the core principle that distinguishes a well-functioning military from a disorganised and ineffective one. A military that operates according to a high standard of professionalism is one that values discipline, competence, and ethical conduct. However, when poor leadership prevails, professionalism begins to erode. Bad Generals who fail to uphold the standards of the military, whether through negligence or corruption, set a precedent that undermines the institution's entire ethos.

The erosion of professionalism manifests in various ways. It can be seen in the rise of sloppy, ineffective training, where soldiers are not properly prepared for combat or leadership challenges. It can also be seen in the decline of attention to detail, where operational standards slip and missions are executed with less precision and care. In the worst cases, poor leadership leads to a complete breakdown of discipline, where soldiers no longer feel the need to adhere to established norms or protocols. This decline in professionalism can result in catastrophic failure in operations, loss of life, and a complete breakdown of military effectiveness.

Bad leadership also leads to the neglect of the military's ethical and moral code. A General who tolerates unethical behaviour or engages in morally questionable actions sets a precedent for the entire institution. Soldiers who see their leaders engaging in such behaviour may begin to view it as acceptable.

THE VERY VERY BEST BAD 4-STAR GENERAL

This leads to a culture of moral compromise within the ranks. Over time, this diminishes the military's ability to function as an ethical force, weakening its ability to carry out its duties with honour and integrity. The loss of professionalism diminishes the military's standing, both internally and externally, and reduces its ability to maintain order and command respect.

The most dangerous aspect of poor leadership is that its consequences are often not immediately visible. The immediate effects are easy to identify, but the long-term costs are more difficult to measure. Bad leadership causes a slow erosion of the military institution's foundational elements, which may not become apparent until years later. The soldiers who serve under a bad General may not realise the full extent of the damage they are experiencing, but future generations of soldiers will bear the brunt of the consequences.

The impact on future generations is profound. The leadership practices of today shape the leaders of tomorrow. Flawed or corrupt practices will create a cycle of poor leadership that is difficult to break. New recruits entering the military may learn bad habits from the current generation of soldiers. This perpetuates a toxic culture and undermines the military's ability to function effectively. Over time, this cycle can lead to an entire generation of soldiers who are unprepared, disengaged, and poorly trained.

Additionally, poor leadership breeds a lack of innovation and adaptability. The military is an institution that must constantly evolve to meet new challenges and threats. However, a military led by bad Generals often becomes stagnant, relying on outdated strategies and tactics that no longer serve the needs of the modern world. This lack of innovation puts future generations at a distinct disadvantage, as they may find themselves ill-prepared to confront new challenges or emerging threats.

In conclusion, the silent costs of poor leadership, corruption, loss of trust, and erosion of professionalism are not immediately visible. They have lasting effects that can devastate a military institution. The gradual decline in standards, morale, and cohesion undermines the military's capacity to function effectively and prepare for future challenges. Rebuilding after such damage is a monumental task, requiring a cultural shift, a return to ethical leadership, and a deep commitment to restoring the trust and professionalism that were lost. However, the damage caused by poor leadership is not irreversible, and with the right leadership in place, it is possible to rebuild and restore the military to its former strength. The key is to learn from past mistakes and prepare future leaders to uphold the values that keep the military strong, ethical, and ready for future challenges.

*

CHAPTER 13

THE PSYCHOLOGY OF LEADERSHIP: THE POWER OF CONFIDENCE VERSUS HUBRIS

Leadership in the military, as in any field, is not simply a matter of strategy, tactics, or operational skill. It is deeply rooted in psychological dynamics. The most successful military leaders understand that their actions, decisions, and demeanour significantly influence the morale and effectiveness of their troops. Confidence and arrogance are two sides of the same psychological coin. How a leader balances these traits can determine the lives of soldiers and the success of military operations. This chapter explores the delicate psychological balance between confidence and hubris in military leadership, examining how the best leaders maintain a humble, empathetic approach, while the worst succumb to self-absorption, arrogance, and a disregard for their limitations.

Confidence is an essential quality in any military leader. A leader must be self-assured in their decisions, providing direction, support, and motivation for the troops in high-pressure situations. Confidence inspires trust and respect from subordinates, creating a sense of stability and certainty within the ranks. When soldiers see their leader approach challenges with determination and clarity, they are more likely to follow orders with conviction, knowing the leader is capable of navigating the complexities of the battlefield. Confidence is contagious; it encourages soldiers to believe in themselves and their mission.

However, confidence must be tempered with humility. A good leader understands that they do not have all the answers and that the success of a military operation often hinges on collective effort and input. They seek advice, listen to their subordinates, and are open to feedback. They recognise that their decisions, while confident, are based on the expertise and contributions of others. A good leader is aware of their limits and is not afraid to admit when they are unsure or need help. This humility fosters an environment of mutual respect and collaboration, where soldiers feel valued and empowered to contribute their insights.

Hubris, on the other hand, is the dark side of confidence. It is an overblown sense of self-importance that leads a leader to believe they are invincible, infallible, and superior to others. Arrogance often results from an inflated ego, a sense of entitlement, or a deep-seated need for personal validation. When a leader falls into the trap of hubris, they begin to make decisions without considering the input of others, dismissing the expertise and advice of subordinates. Overconfidence often blinds them to risks and obstacles, leading to reckless decisions that can have catastrophic consequences.

Hubris is dangerous because it distorts a leader's perception of reality. A leader blinded by arrogance may miscalculate the enemy's strength, underestimate their own forces' capabilities, or fail to adapt to changing circumstances. Furthermore, they may become more focused on their own image and legacy than on the welfare of the soldiers or the mission's success. In military leadership, where lives are at stake, hubris is often the difference between victory and defeat, life and death.

The psychological dynamics between confidence and arrogance are critical; they define the trajectory of a military campaign and the well-being of the soldiers under a leader's command.

The most effective military leaders demonstrate humility, empathy, and self-awareness in their leadership style. Humility allows them to recognise that they are not infallible and that their decisions are only as good as the information and counsel they receive from their subordinates. It enables them to remain open to learning and self-improvement, which is essential for growth and development as a leader. A humble leader knows that rank and position do not make them superior to others, but instead give them the responsibility to serve and guide their troops.

Empathy is another key quality that distinguishes great leaders from their less effective counterparts. A leader with empathy understands the emotional and psychological needs of their soldiers. They recognise the toll that war takes on the mind and body and show a genuine concern for their troops' well-being. Empathy fosters strong relationships within the unit, as soldiers feel supported, valued, and understood. This emotional connection between leaders and troops strengthens loyalty and trust, which are critical components of military success. An empathetic leader can recognise stress, burnout, or trauma in soldiers and act early to protect the unit's effectiveness.

Self-awareness is the third pillar of good leadership. A self-aware leader understands their strengths and weaknesses, as well as the psychological and emotional factors that influence their decision-making. They are cognizant of how their actions and character affect their troops, and they work to model the behaviours and values they wish to see in others. Self-awareness allows a leader to avoid the pitfalls of ego and arrogance, enabling them to objectively assess their own performance and adjust when necessary.

It also enables them to stay grounded, even in high-pressure situations, preventing them from being swept up in the illusions of grandeur that often accompany positions of power.

Together, humility, empathy, and self-awareness form the foundation of effective leadership. These qualities help a leader build trust, make informed decisions, and apply emotional intelligence in complex military operations. Leaders with these qualities achieve battlefield success while building a lasting culture of trust, respect, and collaboration.

While good leadership requires confidence, humility, empathy, and self-awareness, it is important to acknowledge that leadership, particularly in the military, is a psychologically demanding role. Military leaders face immense pressure to make life-and-death decisions, often with limited information and under extreme time constraints. The psychological toll of this responsibility can manifest as stress, isolation, and a distorted sense of ego.

The stress that comes with leadership can be overwhelming. Military leaders are responsible for the lives of their soldiers, and the weight of that responsibility can lead to anxiety, burnout, and even PTSD. Leaders who fail to manage their stress may become less effective in their decision-making, losing clarity of thought and their ability to lead with confidence. Leadership stress can cause emotional detachment, making leaders prioritise the mission and organisation over troop well-being. This emotional distance can erode the trust and loyalty between leaders and soldiers, making it harder to maintain a cohesive and motivated unit.

Isolation is another psychological challenge that military leaders often face. As they rise through the ranks, leaders are often separated from their subordinates, spending more time with their peers or superiors than with the soldiers they lead.

This isolation can make it difficult for leaders to stay connected with the realities of frontline service. Without regular interaction with the troops, leaders may lose touch with their soldiers' daily struggles, concerns, and experiences. This lack of connection can lead to a breakdown in communication and an inability to respond to the unit's needs effectively. Additionally, the isolation of leadership can create a sense of loneliness, where the leader feels burdened by the weight of their decisions and cut off from the support of their comrades.

At the same time, the power and authority that come with leadership can lead to an inflated sense of ego. Leaders who are not mindful of their psychological well-being may begin to believe that their rank and authority make them superior to others. An inflated ego can skew decisions, prioritising image or legacy over soldiers' welfare and mission success. It can also make it difficult for a leader to accept criticism or feedback, further isolating them from the very people who could help them make better decisions.

When a leader's ego goes unchecked, the consequences can be catastrophic, both on and off the battlefield. Excessive ego leads to arrogance, which clouds judgment and prevents a leader from accurately assessing risks and opportunities. A leader blinded by their own self-importance is less likely to listen to their subordinates, consider alternative perspectives, or make necessary adjustments in the face of changing circumstances.

On the battlefield, a leader with an excessive ego may fail to recognise the strengths and weaknesses of both their own forces and the enemy. They may underestimate the capabilities of the opposing side, leading to strategic miscalculations that result in unnecessary losses. A leader who is overly confident in their own abilities may also refuse to adapt to their tactics, clinging to outdated strategies even when they are no longer effective.

THE VERY VERY BEST BAD 4-STAR GENERAL

This refusal to acknowledge the limits of one's knowledge or experience can lead to devastating outcomes. Off the battlefield, excessive ego can damage the leader's relationships with their peers, superiors, and subordinates. A leader who is arrogant and self-absorbed may alienate key members of their team, creating a toxic environment where collaboration and trust are absent. This lack of cooperation can lead to poor decision-making, inefficiency, and a decline in overall unit cohesion. In extreme cases, a leader's ego can drive corruption, prioritising personal power and interests over the mission and their soldiers.

In conclusion, the psychology of leadership in the military is complex and multifaceted, requiring a balance of confidence with an awareness of the danger of arrogance. The best leaders are those who maintain a sense of humility, empathy, and self-awareness, allowing them to inspire loyalty, trust, and effective teamwork. These leaders understand the psychological toll that leadership can take and work to manage their stress, maintain connections with their troops, and avoid the pitfalls of excessive ego. By recognising the fine line between confidence and hubris, military leaders can avoid the catastrophic consequences of poor decision-making and create an environment where soldiers feel supported, motivated, and empowered. Leadership, at its best, is not about asserting power over others but about serving the greater good and leading with integrity, humility, and wisdom.

*

CHAPTER 14

LEADING IN DIVERSITY: EMBRACING STRENGTH IN DIFFERENCES

Diversity is often seen as a challenge in organisations, particularly in military settings where cohesion and unity are vital to operational success. However, when effectively managed, diversity can be one of the greatest assets a military leader can leverage. In the context of military leadership, diversity refers to the inclusion of individuals with varying backgrounds, perspectives, and experiences. This includes, but is not limited to, cultural, gender, and intellectual diversity. Embracing diversity in the ranks is not just a matter of equity or morality; it is a strategic advantage that can enhance problem-solving, adaptability, and decision-making. This chapter explores the importance of recognising and embracing diversity within military ranks and how leaders who foster an inclusive environment can turn differences into strengths. It also highlights how bad leadership misuses diversity by suppressing, ignoring, or weaponising it, thereby creating a toxic culture that weakens the military.

A diverse military brings together different perspectives and solutions, fostering innovation and adaptability. Leaders who harness this diversity make stronger, well-rounded decisions that increase the chances of success.

Diversity in a military context can take many forms: cultural, gender, educational, socioeconomic, and even experiential. Cultural diversity introduces different ways of thinking, communicating, and solving problems shaped by varied historical, social, and geographical contexts. A culturally aware military leader can better understand and manage these differences, ensuring that each soldier's unique perspective is valued and respected.

Gender diversity is another important aspect of modern military organisations. Many armed forces have historically been male-dominated. The inclusion of women in the military is both a matter of fairness and an operational necessity. Female soldiers bring different strengths to the table, from unique communication styles to the ability to provide a fresh perspective on problem-solving. Leaders who foster an environment where both men and women are equally represented and respected can benefit from a broader pool of talent and viewpoints.

Intellectual diversity refers to the range of educational backgrounds, professional experiences, and areas of expertise that individuals bring to the military. While many soldiers may have similar training and technical skills, they may also have different academic disciplines or personal experiences that contribute to their problem-solving abilities. A military leader who recognises the value of intellectual diversity is more likely to tap into these varied skill sets, fostering a culture of learning, creativity, and strategic thinking.

When a leader leverages the diverse strengths of their troops, they create a more agile, innovative, and resilient force. Diversity creates a rich environment where soldiers learn, challenge assumptions, and grow together.

A good leader actively embraces it as a source of strength, not just something to tolerate. Leveraging diversity starts with an inclusive environment where all soldiers feel respected, valued, and supported. True inclusivity ensures everyone can contribute, recognising diversity as a source of strength, not a liability.

A good leader fosters inclusivity by setting the tone from the top, modelling respectful behaviour, and ensuring that all soldiers have an equal voice. Leaders should actively encourage open dialogue, creating a space where soldiers feel comfortable sharing their ideas, concerns, and experiences. This is crucial for creating an environment where minorities feel their contributions are recognised and valued. In an inclusive military, leaders actively seek out diverse viewpoints when making decisions. They understand that a homogenous group, while potentially more cohesive, can also fall prey to groupthink and a lack of creativity. By seeking input from individuals with varying perspectives, leaders are more likely to make well-rounded decisions that account for a range of factors and considerations. Inclusivity also means providing equal opportunities for professional development, ensuring that all soldiers have access to the same resources, mentorship, and advancement opportunities.

Moreover, leaders must recognise that inclusivity is not just about numbers; it is about creating a culture where every individual feels that they belong and are integral to the mission's success. This requires a commitment to diversity and inclusivity at all levels of the organisation, from recruitment and training to promotions and assignments. It is essential for military leaders to continuously assess their unit's culture to ensure that all members feel they have a stake in the unit's success and that their contributions are valued.

When leadership overlooks diversity, it stifles innovation, lowers morale, and fosters a toxic culture. In the military, where unity is vital, ignoring inclusion can weaken the fabric of the unit.

One of the most damaging effects of bad leadership is the creation of a homogenous and exclusionary culture. In such an environment, soldiers who do not conform to the dominant culture may feel alienated, isolated, or marginalised. This can lead to reduced motivation, lower job satisfaction, and even desertion or insubordination. Soldiers who feel their unique backgrounds and perspectives are not valued may disengage from their duties, leading to decreased productivity and morale.

Furthermore, a lack of diversity can result in poor decision-making. Leaders who rely on a narrow pool of similar experiences and viewpoints are more likely to make decisions that are short-sighted or uninformed. Groupthink can take hold, where the desire for uniformity and consensus overrides critical thinking and innovation. In military operations, where adaptability and strategic thinking are crucial, this kind of decision-making can be catastrophic.

The suppression of diversity can also have long-term consequences for the military institution. When certain groups are systematically excluded, whether based on gender, race, or other factors, the military loses out on a wealth of talent and potential. Over time, this exclusionary culture can perpetuate itself, creating a self-reinforcing cycle where new recruits are discouraged from joining or staying in the military, leading to a lack of diversity in future generations.

Moreover, when diversity is weaponised to divide or pit groups against each other, it can create deep cracks within the military. Leaders who use identity politics or cater to certain groups while neglecting others foster antipathy and distrust. This divisiveness erodes morale, undermines unit cohesion, and creates a toxic environment where loyalty and trust are in short supply. In extreme cases, this kind of leadership can lead to mutiny, insubordination, or the collapse of a unit's ability to function effectively.

THE VERY VERY BEST BAD 4-STAR GENERAL

Case Studies

Throughout history, there have been numerous examples where bad leadership and the failure to embrace diversity led to disastrous consequences. In World War II, for instance, the German military's rigid, hierarchical structure and strict cultural homogeneity contributed to its downfall. Despite the country's military prowess, the lack of diversity in thought and strategy left the German army ill-prepared for the changing dynamics of the battlefield. Hitler's refusal to accept differing viewpoints and his reliance on sycophantic officers led to critical strategic errors, particularly in the Soviet campaign, which ultimately resulted in a costly defeat.

The U.S. military's integration of women and minorities highlights the importance of diversity. Despite progress in inclusivity, early resistance created divisions and reduced effectiveness; the exclusion of women from combat roles harmed morale and limited valuable contributions. Over time, however, leaders who embraced inclusivity recognised that a diverse force strengthened the military's overall effectiveness. Policy changes were made to open doors for all qualified soldiers, regardless of gender or ethnicity.

In Eswatini's defence force, institutional decline has become evident, driven by a lack of leadership diversity, limited inclusivity, and resistance to merit-based advancement. Power concentrated in a narrow circle has stifled talent, discouraged initiative, and prioritised compliance over competence. As a result, the force has lost its operational edge, facing weakened morale, internal disillusionment, and an inability to adapt to modern security threats and challenges that inclusive leadership and open dialogue might have prevented.

The failure of leadership to recognise and manage diversity within military ranks can have far-reaching effects that extend beyond the immediate consequences of poor decisions. It can shape the culture of an entire institution, creating lasting damage that can take years, if not decades, to repair. Leaders who fail to appreciate the strength that lies in diversity are essentially blind to one of the most potent tools at their disposal.

The future of military leadership depends on embracing diversity as a strength. Inclusive leaders who respect, value, and empower every soldier build a culture of collaboration, innovation, and resilience. The best leaders understand that the strength of a military force lies not in its uniformity but in its diversity. They value diverse perspectives and experiences, knowing that embracing them strengthens the army and enhances its adaptability. Leaders who embrace diversity actively seek it, recognising it as key to long-term success on and off the battlefield.

On the other hand, leaders who suppress or ignore diversity create a toxic environment that undermines unity, morale, and mission success. The consequences of such leadership are profound, affecting not only the military's immediate effectiveness but also its long-term viability. By failing to leverage diversity, leaders miss out on the strategic advantages that come from a broad range of ideas, perspectives, and talents.

The future of military leadership will depend on leaders' ability to understand and embrace the power of diversity. In a rapidly changing world, where complexity and unpredictability are the norm, the ability to draw strength from differences is not just an advantage; it is a necessity. The leaders who succeed will be those who understand that the richness of their ranks, in all their diversity, is the greatest asset they possess.

*

CHAPTER 15

ACCOUNTABILITY IN LEADERSHIP: ENSURING TRANSPARENCY AND RESPONSIBILITY

Leadership in any field, but especially in the military, hinges on one critical principle: accountability. Whether leading a team, an organisation, or an entire nation's armed forces, a leader's decisions and actions must be guided by a sense of personal responsibility and transparency. Accountability in military leadership is not just about ensuring that orders are followed; it is about taking ownership of the consequences of one's decisions, both good and bad. A leader must be ready to answer for their actions, admit mistakes, and make amends when necessary. This chapter examines the role of accountability in military leadership, showing how strong generals instil it and how its absence breeds dishonesty, secrecy, and blame-shifting. We will also examine case studies of military leaders who faced accountability for their actions and the ripple effects of those decisions.

In the military, accountability is an essential aspect of building trust, maintaining discipline, and fostering unity. Soldiers place their lives in the hands of their commanders, trusting that they will make decisions that safeguard their safety, honour, and dignity.

Accountability ensures that leaders are held responsible for the outcomes of their decisions, fostering an environment of transparency and integrity. In military leadership, accountability is not just about answering to superiors; it is about answering to the soldiers, the institution, and the mission.

Accountability begins with a leader's ability to model personal responsibility. The best generals understand that their authority and credibility are not absolute but are earned through their actions. They take ownership of the decisions they make, even when things go wrong. This openness creates a culture where accountability is woven into the fabric of the organisation. Leaders who demonstrate accountability set the standard for their subordinates, showing them that owning one's actions and admitting mistakes is not a weakness but a mark of strength and integrity.

Furthermore, military leaders who prioritise accountability create a culture of mutual respect and trust. Soldiers who see their commanders owning up to their mistakes are more likely to do the same. This transparency fosters a sense of loyalty and cooperation, ensuring that the mission is not derailed by dishonesty or blame-shifting. Accountability strengthens the bond between officers and their troops, as it creates an environment where everyone, regardless of rank, is held to the same high standard.

In contrast, a lack of accountability can unravel the very fabric of military cohesion. A culture that lacks accountability is one where blame is deflected, dishonesty flourishes, and leadership becomes reactive rather than proactive. When leaders fail to take responsibility for their actions, they set a dangerous precedent for their subordinates, encouraging a culture of finger-pointing and avoiding responsibility. This erosion of accountability can lead to systemic problems, undermining the effectiveness and morale of the entire organisation.

The best generals understand that accountability is a core value that must be instilled in their subordinates at every level of the military. They organisation that it is not enough to simply demand accountability; they must create systems and cultures that encourage it and make it an intrinsic part of military life.

One key way that effective leaders instil accountability is by setting clear expectations and standards. Soldiers must know what is expected of them and understand the consequences of not meeting those expectations. The best generals ensure that accountability is embedded into the daily operations of the military. This begins with clear communication of objectives, timelines, and roles. By setting these clear expectations, leaders provide a framework within which accountability can thrive.

In addition to clarity, the best generals foster an environment where subordinates are encouraged to take initiative and ownership of their tasks. They empower their soldiers to make decisions and solve problems while also making it clear that they will be held responsible for the outcomes. This sense of ownership breeds a culture of accountability where soldiers take pride in their work and understand the consequences of both success and failure.

Accountability is also instilled through consistent and fair discipline. The best generals understand that accountability is not about punishment, but about fairness and consistency. When mistakes are made, they are dealt with in a manner that is just and corrective, not vindictive. Soldiers are held accountable for their actions, but they are also given the support and guidance needed to learn from their mistakes and improve. By holding their subordinates to high standards and treating them with respect, great leaders ensure that accountability is seen as a positive force within the organisation.

THE VERY VERY BEST BAD 4-STAR GENERAL

The best generals lead by example. They demonstrate accountability in their own actions, showing their troops that they are not exempt from responsibility. This sets the tone for the entire organisation, creating a culture where accountability is seen as a fundamental part of leadership, not a burden to be avoided. When a leader admits their mistakes and takes corrective action, it sends a powerful message to subordinates that accountability is valued and essential to the success of the mission.

In stark contrast to effective leadership, bad generals often avoid responsibility and deflect blame for their actions. These leaders refuse to admit mistakes, shift blame onto others and prioritise self-preservation over their troops and the mission. The avoidance of accountability can have disastrous consequences for both the leader and the organisation they command.

One of the hallmark traits of bad generals is a tendency to deflect blame. When things go wrong, these leaders often point fingers at their subordinates, external factors, or even their superiors, rather than taking responsibility for their own role in the situation. This lack of accountability creates an atmosphere of distrust and disillusionment within the ranks. Soldiers who see their leaders deflect blame are less likely to take responsibility for their own actions, leading to a cycle of avoidance and dishonesty that permeates the entire organisation.

The refusal to take responsibility can also manifest in the form of arrogance or denial. Bad generals often view themselves as infallible and refuse to acknowledge when they have made mistakes. This ego-driven leadership can result in poor decision-making and a lack of adaptation to changing circumstances. When a leader is unwilling to admit error or take corrective action, the entire organisation suffers.

As a result, subordinates may begin to feel disillusioned, demoralised, and disengaged, leading to lower morale and performance. Moreover, bad generals often create a culture of secrecy and dishonesty. In the absence of transparency, soldiers are left in the dark about key decisions and the reasons behind them. This secrecy breeds suspicion and undermines trust, as soldiers feel that they are not being given the full picture. When soldiers cannot trust their leaders, their commitment to the mission and the organisation diminishes. A lack of transparency also leads to a breakdown in communication, making it difficult for subordinates to understand the larger strategic vision and their role within it.

The culture of dishonesty and secrecy that bad generals foster is not limited to the leadership level; it extends throughout the entire organisation. When soldiers see their leaders lying or covering up mistakes, they are more likely to do the same. This creates a toxic environment where accountability is avoided at all costs, leading to poor decision-making, unethical behaviour, and a lack of operational readiness.

Case Studies

Throughout history, there have been numerous examples of military leaders who were forced to face the consequences of their actions. In some cases, this accountability came in the form of public humiliation, demotion, or even court-martial. These case studies illustrate the importance of accountability in military leadership and the ripple effects of decisions made by those in positions of power.

One prominent example is General William Westmoreland, who commanded U.S. forces during the Vietnam War. Westmoreland was widely criticised for his handling of the war, particularly for his insistence on a strategy of attrition.

This strategy focused on killing large numbers of enemy soldiers in an effort to break the will of the North Vietnamese. The strategy ultimately proved ineffective, leading to widespread public dissatisfaction with the war effort and Westmoreland's leadership. Though he was not held personally accountable for the war's outcome, his reputation was tarnished, and his credibility as a military leader was severely damaged. His failure to take responsibility for the failure of his strategy and the mounting casualties led to a loss of trust in his leadership.

Another example is the case of General George McClellan, the commander of the Union Army during the American Civil War. McClellan was known for his reluctance to engage the enemy and his inability to take decisive action, despite having a large and well-equipped army at his disposal. His failure to act led to missed opportunities and unnecessary losses, ultimately resulting in his removal from command by President Abraham Lincoln. McClellan's reluctance to take responsibility for his failure to achieve victories, coupled with his tendency to blame others for his mistakes, made him a controversial figure in American military history. His inability to accept accountability for his decisions and his failure to learn from his mistakes were key factors in his eventual downfall.

In more recent history, General Stanley McChrystal's leadership in Afghanistan provides another example of the importance of accountability. McChrystal was highly regarded for his leadership and innovative approach to counterinsurgency warfare. However, his downfall came when a report in *Rolling Stone* magazine revealed that McChrystal and his staff had made disparaging remarks about President Barack Obama and other senior officials. Though the comments were not made in a professional setting, they violated the principles of military discipline and accountability. McChrystal was held accountable for his actions and ultimately resigned from his position. This demonstrates that no leader, no matter how esteemed, is exempt from the need to be accountable for their conduct.

Within the Kingdom of Eswatini, General Jeffery Tshabalala, a senior military officer, chose to step down following mounting public pressure after a pronouncement was leaked and published by an online news outlet. Though the statement in question was believed to be part of internal military discourse, the fact that it became public raised concerns about civil-military relations, strategic discipline, and the ethical responsibilities of high-ranking officers.

In clarifying his decision, General Tshabalala emphasised that he did not resign from the Defence Force but made a decision to vacate his seat for the purpose of making peace. He further stated that had he not already reached his retirement age, he would have requested early retirement. What transpired in his life, as he explained, occurred under duress, and for that reason, he deserved to be treated as a retired general. By recognising the importance of preserving the credibility and professional image of the Defence Force, he vacated the position. His decision, though painful, was widely seen as an act of integrity and professionalism. It restored a measure of public confidence in the armed forces and set a precedent for ethical leadership.

In stark contrast, his successor faced multiple allegations of corruption and misconduct, some of which were also exposed through the same online news publication. Reports included nepotism in promotions, misuse of military resources, and fostering a culture of fear and silence within the ranks. Despite the gravity of these allegations and growing internal unrest, he refused to step down.

Instead, he clung to his position, allegedly relying on political connections and traditional networks to shield him from accountability. His continued presence at the helm contributed to deteriorating morale, further divisions among officers, and a growing perception that impunity had become entrenched in the leadership structure.

When comparing the two cases, General Tshabalala's decision to vacate his position, although personally costly, is remembered as a dignified and courageous act that prioritised institutional integrity over individual ambition. His decision, though taken under duress, prevented further reputational damage to the military and inspired a culture of responsibility among subordinate commanders. Conversely, his successor's refusal to step aside, despite serious allegations, is cited as a textbook example of leadership failure, where personal preservation was valued above service ethos and national interest. Both cases offer powerful lessons. While one leader bowed out to protect the institution, the other undermined it by prioritising self-interest.

Together, they underscore the principle that accountability remains a cornerstone of credible military leadership. The military, by nature, must be anchored in discipline, integrity, and loyalty, not to personalities, but to the state and its people. These case studies demonstrate the far-reaching effects of leadership decisions and the importance of accountability in maintaining trust, cohesion, and operational effectiveness. The failure to take responsibility for one's actions can lead to a loss of credibility, trust, and respect, both within the military and among the public.

In conclusion, accountability is one of the most important aspects of military leadership. It is the cornerstone of trust, discipline, and unity, ensuring that leaders take ownership of their actions and decisions. The best generals understand that accountability is not just about personal responsibility; it is about setting an example for their subordinates and creating a culture where responsibility, transparency, and integrity are valued. Bad generals, on the other hand, avoid accountability, deflect blame, and foster a culture of dishonesty and secrecy. This lack of responsibility undermines trust, erodes morale, and weakens the entire organisation.

When leaders fail to take responsibility for their actions, the ripple effects can be felt throughout the military, from the battlefield to the highest echelons of command. Ultimately, accountability is essential for the success of any military operation. Leaders who embrace accountability create an environment where soldiers are empowered to take ownership of their actions, learn from their mistakes, and grow as individuals. In contrast, leaders who avoid responsibility create a toxic culture that undermines the effectiveness and cohesion of the entire organisation. As such, accountability is not just a personal virtue; it is a strategic necessity for success in military leadership.

*

CHAPTER 16

THE IMPACT OF LEADERSHIP ON CIVIL-MILITARY RELATIONS

The relationship between the military and the civilian government is one of the most critical elements of a nation's stability. Throughout history, the impact of military leadership on civil-military relations has been profound, influencing everything from national security to social stability. A general's leadership style, values, and ethical standards can either strengthen the bonds between the military and civilian institutions or create rifts that lead to distrust, conflict, and even instability. This chapter delves into the ways military leadership shapes civil-military relations, focusing on the importance of ethical leadership in maintaining trust and preventing negative consequences, such as civil unrest, military coups, or societal breakdown.

At its core, civil-military relations are defined by the balance of power, authority, and responsibility between military leaders and civilian authorities. In a healthy, functional society, the military serves as an instrument of national defence, charged with protecting the nation from external threats. The civilian government, on the other hand, provides political direction, strategic oversight, and the legal framework under which the military operates.

This division of power ensures that the military remains subordinate to civilian leadership, preventing the risk of military rule or undue influence on governance.

However, the relationship between the military and the civilian government is not always straightforward. In some countries, military leaders wield substantial political power, often to the point of undermining the authority of elected civilian officials. In these contexts, military leaders may bypass civilian oversight, undermine democratic processes, or even take control of the government through coups or insurrection. Conversely, a strong and ethical military leader who maintains respect for civilian authority can help strengthen democracy and build public trust in both the military and the government.

A general's leadership is central to this dynamic. The way a leader interacts with civilian officials, the respect they show for civilian institutions, and their commitment to upholding democratic values can significantly impact the relationship between the military and the broader society. Generals who understand their role within the framework of a democratic society tend to reinforce the importance of civilian control, while those who lack this understanding can weaken the checks and balances that ensure the military does not overstep its bounds.

Ethical leadership is perhaps the most significant factor in maintaining healthy civil-military relations. Ethical generals understand that the military's primary role is to defend the nation and protect the welfare of its citizens, not to pursue personal or political gain. These leaders prioritise integrity, transparency, and respect for democratic values. They recognise that their actions have a direct impact on the public's perception of the military and its relationship with the civilian government.

When military leaders act ethically, they help build trust between the armed forces and the broader society. The public must have confidence that the military is not only capable of defending the nation but also committed to acting within the bounds of the law and respecting civilian governance. Ethical leadership fosters this trust by demonstrating a commitment to professionalism, respect for human rights, and accountability in both military operations and internal affairs.

A general who upholds ethical leadership also ensures that the military remains apolitical. The military must never be used as a tool to further partisan or personal interests, as this undermines public confidence and could lead to dangerous political interference. Ethical generals recognise that military service is about duty to the nation, not allegiance to any political party or ideology. By maintaining an apolitical stance and working in harmony with civilian authorities, ethical leaders help preserve the integrity of both the military and the political system.

Moreover, ethical leadership in the military has a ripple effect that extends to the rank and file. Soldiers are influenced by their commanders' actions, and a strong ethical foundation instils a sense of responsibility and honour throughout the military. When soldiers see their leaders adhering to high ethical standards, they are more likely to emulate those values. This ensures that the military as a whole remains a trusted institution.

In contrast, when generals fail to demonstrate ethical leadership, they risk damaging the relationship between the military and the public. A lack of ethics can create divisions within the armed forces, where soldiers may feel disillusioned, demoralised, or distrustful of their leadership. Furthermore, unethical actions, such as corruption, abuse of power, or political manipulation, can erode public trust in the military, leading to a loss of credibility and respect.

While ethical leadership strengthens civil-military relations, the opposite is true for corrupt or misguided generals. Generals who abuse their position, engage in corrupt practices, or pursue personal or political agendas undermine the very foundation of trust that holds the military and civilian government together. Such leadership can have far-reaching consequences, including the breakdown of societal order, civil unrest, or even military coups.

Corrupt generals are often more concerned with advancing their own interests than fulfilling their duty to the nation. They may use the military as a vehicle for personal wealth, power, or influence, engaging in illegal activities such as misappropriation, bribery, or illicit arms deals. This corruption weakens the military's ability to perform its duties effectively and damages its reputation in the eyes of the public. When the public becomes aware of military corruption, trust in the institution erodes, and civil-military relations are severely strained.

Furthermore, a corrupt or misguided general may become entangled in political power struggles, using the military as a tool for political manipulation. These leaders may attempt to undermine civilian authority by aligning with political factions, exerting pressure on the government, or even staging a coup to seize power. The consequences of such actions can be devastating, leading to political instability, economic decline, and a breakdown in social cohesion. When the military intervenes in politics, it risks losing legitimacy, appearing as a tool of corrupt or authoritarian rule rather than a defender of democracy and the constitution.

In some cases, the breakdown of civil-military relations due to corrupt leadership can fuel civil unrest. When military leaders act in ways that are perceived as self-serving or unjust, public dissatisfaction can grow, leading to protests, strikes, or even violent uprisings.

The military, in turn, may be called upon to quell these disturbances, often using force to maintain order. This can lead to a cycle of violence and repression, with the military becoming increasingly separated from the population it is supposed to protect.

Perhaps the most extreme consequence of poor leadership is the military coup. When a general disregards civilian authority or engages in corrupt activities, it can lead to a loss of confidence in the military's commitment to the nation's democratic values. In such cases, factions within the military may decide that the only way to restore order is to seize power, overthrowing the government and establishing military rule. History is filled with examples of military coups triggered by leadership failures, and the impact of such events on civil-military relations is profound. A coup can result in the collapse of democratic institutions, the rise of authoritarian regimes, and a significant loss of public trust in the military.

The failure of military leadership to maintain ethical standards not only weakens civil-military relations but can also contribute to the breakdown of societal order. The military, when misled by corrupt or misguided leaders, may become a destabilising force rather than a stabilising one. In the absence of strong leadership, the military may become divided, ineffective, or prone to manipulation, which can leave a nation vulnerable to external threats and internal turmoil.

When the military is not trusted by the civilian population, the entire societal fabric begins to deteriorate. Citizens may begin to question the legitimacy of the state and its institutions, including the military. If the military becomes a symbol of corruption or oppression, citizens may view it as an enemy rather than a protector. This sense of division can erode national unity and create deep divides within society, making it difficult to address collective challenges or build a cohesive national identity.

Moreover, a breakdown in civil-military relations can lead to the weakening of democratic norms and institutions. When the military becomes politicised or disconnected from civilian oversight, it may act as a force of repression rather than protection. In extreme cases, military-led regimes may dismantle democratic institutions, suppress political opposition, and curtail civil liberties. This erosion of democratic values can result in long-term social and political consequences, including a loss of personal freedom, widespread poverty, and diminished international credibility.

In conclusion, the relationship between the military and civilian government is one of the most important elements of a nation's stability. A general's leadership style plays a pivotal role in shaping this relationship, influencing everything from public trust in the military to the functioning of democratic institutions. Ethical leadership builds trust and integrity, while corrupt leadership risks unrest, coups, and societal collapse. As history has shown, the consequences of poor leadership in the military are far-reaching and can lead to profound instability.

The best generals understand the importance of their role not only as military leaders but as stewards of the nation's democratic values. By upholding ethical standards, prioritising transparency, and respecting civilian authority, they strengthen civil-military relations and ensure that the military remains a force for good in society. When military leaders fail to uphold these principles, however, the entire nation suffers. Thus, leadership in the military is not just about strategy and tactics; it is about preserving the very fabric of society itself.

*

CHAPTER 17

THE ROLE OF TECHNOLOGY AND INNOVATION IN MODERN MILITARY LEADERSHIP

The nature of warfare has undergone profound changes in recent decades, driven by rapid technological advancements that have transformed the battlefield into ways once unimaginable. Modern military leaders face the challenge of adapting to a landscape where technology increasingly shapes strategy, operations, and combat itself. This chapter explores the crucial role of technology and innovation in modern military leadership. It examines how leaders can embrace and adapt to technological advances such as artificial intelligence (AI), cybersecurity, unmanned systems, and other emerging capabilities.

Additionally, this chapter discusses the detrimental consequences of a general's failure to innovate and adapt to these technologies, as well as the success stories of leaders who have demonstrated foresight and vision. It will also consider how military leaders can balance traditional warfare strategies with the integration of new technological capabilities to ensure that the essence of military leadership remains intact in a rapidly changing landscape.

Warfare has expanded beyond traditional combat, with information technology, AI, unmanned systems, and cyber capabilities reshaping operations. These tools enable precision, efficiency, and real-time intelligence, from UAV surveillance to targeted strikes. Modern leaders must understand and integrate such technologies into their strategy, ensuring they enhance rather than undermine traditional strengths. Artificial Intelligence (AI) is transforming modern warfare by rapidly processing vast amounts of data to provide real-time analysis of battlefield conditions, enemy movements, and logistical challenges. AI supports commanders in decision-making, helping to identify threats, optimise resources, and predict enemy actions with greater accuracy. However, its integration raises concerns about autonomy, accountability, and unintended consequences.

Cybersecurity has likewise become a critical focus. With military operations reliant on interconnected systems, vulnerabilities to cyber-attacks pose serious risks from crippling communications to disrupting supply chains and disabling weapons. Leaders must strengthen defences while also developing offensive capabilities to counter enemy operations.

Unmanned systems, such as UAVs and UGVs, have enhanced operational flexibility and reduced risks to soldiers. They enable surveillance, intelligence gathering, precision strikes, and logistics support. Yet, their growing use raises ethical and operational concerns, including over-reliance on technology and the risks posed by autonomous weapon systems.

While technology strengthens military operations, leaders who cling to outdated strategies risk falling behind. Failure to adapt can lead to unrecognised threats, poor execution, and unpreparedness for future challenges. A prime example of the dangers of failing to innovate can be seen in the military's initial response to the rise of cyber threats.

In the early stages of the internet and digital warfare, many military leaders dismissed the significance of cybersecurity, focusing instead on traditional military threats. As cyber-attacks became more frequent and sophisticated, some militaries were ill-equipped to defend against them, leading to significant vulnerabilities. Countries with leaders who failed to recognise the importance of cybersecurity were caught off guard by attacks that crippled military communications and infrastructure. In contrast, nations that took proactive steps to build robust cyber defence capabilities have been able to maintain operational continuity and adapt to the changing nature of warfare.

Another example of a failure to innovate can be seen in the military's initial hesitance to fully integrate unmanned systems into combat operations. For years, many military leaders underestimated the potential of UAVs and other unmanned platforms, relying instead on manned aircraft and ground forces to carry out surveillance and strike missions. This reluctance to embrace unmanned systems resulted in missed opportunities to enhance operational efficiency, reduce risk to human lives, and improve the precision of military strikes. It wasn't until militaries began to recognise the potential advantages of UAVs that their integration into operations became widespread, marking a shift toward more technologically advanced warfare.

In some cases, generals who fail to innovate may also struggle with the implementation of AI and data analytics. AI-driven systems can analyse vast amounts of data in real time, providing military leaders with insights that can inform strategic decisions. However, leaders who lack the foresight to incorporate AI into their decision-making processes may find themselves relying on outdated methods of intelligence analysis.

This puts them at a disadvantage on the battlefield. The failure to adapt to AI and data analytics can also lead to missed opportunities for optimising resource allocation, logistics, and personnel management. Ultimately, the failure to innovate and adapt to emerging technologies can undermine a military's effectiveness, leaving it vulnerable to modern threats and ill-prepared for future challenges. A general who resists change not only risks losing a competitive advantage but also jeopardises the safety and security of their forces and the nation they serve.

Leaders who embrace innovation and lead with foresight can greatly strengthen military capabilities, using technology to enhance effectiveness, decision-making, and success without undermining traditional values.

One example of forward-thinking leadership can be seen in the success of militaries that have embraced artificial intelligence. Military leaders who integrate AI into their decision-making processes can gain a strategic edge by anticipating adversary movements, predicting outcomes, and optimising resources. These leaders understand that AI is not a substitute for human judgment but a tool that can augment their decision-making capabilities. By leveraging AI to its fullest potential, they can maintain a technological advantage over adversaries who fail to adopt these innovations.

Similarly, military leaders who prioritise cybersecurity have demonstrated foresight in preparing their forces for the challenges of modern warfare. Cybersecurity is now a vital part of national defence, with leaders investing in robust systems, training personnel in cyber warfare, and developing tools to disrupt enemy networks. By recognising the importance of cybersecurity early on, these leaders ensure their military remains resilient in the face of cyber threats, thereby minimising the risk of attacks that could cripple military operations.

The integration of unmanned systems into military operations is another example of leadership success in the face of technological change. Generals who have championed the use of UAVs and UGVs have been able to reduce the risk to human lives, improve the precision of strikes, and gather critical intelligence without exposing personnel to unnecessary danger. These leaders have embraced the potential of unmanned systems, integrating them seamlessly into military operations to achieve tactical and strategic objectives. By investing in these technologies, they have created more flexible, agile, and effective fighting forces capable of responding to the challenges of modern warfare.

While technological advancements have transformed the nature of warfare, military leaders must also recognise the value of traditional strategies and tactics. The key to success in modern warfare lies not in abandoning traditional military principles but in integrating them with new technological capabilities. The most successful generals are those who understand how to balance innovation with the timeless principles of warfare, such as strategy, leadership, and discipline.

While unmanned systems and AI enhance reconnaissance, precision, and insights, they cannot replace skilled human commanders who adapt, make judgment calls, inspire troops, and maintain morale. Technology must complement, not replace, the central role of human leadership in military operations. Generals who balance tradition and innovation use technology to enhance operations without replacing skilled leadership, strategy, or adaptability. They equip their forces with modern tools while emphasising training, discipline, and teamwork, thereby maximising the potential of both personnel and technology.

In conclusion, as technology continues to shape the future of warfare, military leaders must be prepared to embrace innovation and adapt to new realities. The successful general of the future will be one who recognises the potential of emerging technologies, such as AI, cybersecurity, and unmanned systems, and integrates them into military strategy and operations. At the same time, they must balance these advancements with traditional military values and leadership principles to ensure that technology enhances rather than replaces the human element of warfare. Failure to adapt to technology leaves a military vulnerable, while forward-thinking leaders who embrace innovation build agile and efficient forces. Future military leadership will rely on both technological proficiency and the ability to inspire and guide troops in a high-tech environment.

*

CHAPTER 18

LEADERSHIP THROUGH CRISIS: MANAGING CHAOS AND UNCERTAINTY

Crisis is a defining feature of military leadership. It is in times of extreme stress and uncertainty that the true measure of a leader is revealed. Whether on the battlefield or in a broader political or organisational context. A leader's ability to remain calm, focused, and decisive in the face of crisis is what ultimately determines the outcome. This chapter delves into how the best Generals manage chaos and uncertainty, examining the ways in which their leadership during times of crisis shapes the course of events.

At the same time, it explores the challenges faced by ineffective Generals who falter under pressure, making irrational decisions that often worsen the situation. Through the lens of historical examples, we will analyse both successful crisis management and catastrophic failure, shedding light on the critical role that leadership plays in navigating turbulent times.

A military leadership crisis can arise from battlefield surprises, communication failures, political shifts, or collapsing strategies. Such unpredictable events demand quick judgment and adaptability, revealing both the strengths and weaknesses of a leader's character.

Crisis situations demand not only technical expertise and strategic understanding but also emotional intelligence. In these moments, the ability to stay calm, think critically, and make decisive choices can mean the difference between success and failure. Good leaders understand the importance of maintaining a steady hand and conveying a sense of stability to their troops. Leaders who falter in moments of crisis risk spreading fear and confusion, undermining the confidence of their soldiers and leading to disarray. This can result in lost battles, failed missions, or even the collapse of entire military operations.

The trademark of great Generals during times of crisis is their ability to remain calm and composed, even in the most chaotic and high-pressure situations. Such leaders understand that panic and indecision are contagious, and they set the tone for their subordinates through their actions, demeanour, and decision-making processes. In the heat of battle or the midst of a political crisis, their ability to remain focused and strategic provides a sense of clarity and direction to those under their command.

General Dwight D. Eisenhower's leadership during World War II is a prime example of how a General can remain calm and decisive in the face of overwhelming odds. As the Supreme Commander of the Allied Expeditionary Force, Eisenhower was responsible for overseeing the planning and execution of the D-Day invasion, one of the largest and most complex military operations in history. In the lead-up to the invasion, Eisenhower faced numerous crises, logistical challenges, unexpected weather conditions, and the uncertainty of whether the invasion would succeed. Despite these challenges, Eisenhower maintained a steady demeanour, making decisive choices that ultimately led to the success of the mission. His ability to manage uncertainty and keep his subordinates focused was key to the Allied victory in Europe.

THE VERY VERY BEST BAD 4-STAR GENERAL

General Colin Powell's leadership during the Gulf War in 1991 exemplified the power of calm and clear decision-making in a high-stress environment. Powell, who served as Chairman of the Joint Chiefs of Staff, remained composed throughout the conflict, guiding military strategy with clarity and purpose. Powell's calm demeanour and willingness to trust in his military commanders allowed for successful coalition operations and a decisive victory over Iraq. His ability to handle the pressures of a rapidly escalating conflict and his strategic foresight were pivotal in achieving the war's objectives with minimal casualties.

In both these examples, the leaders demonstrated the critical ability to maintain their composure, assess situations objectively, and make decisions that inspired confidence in their forces. By managing their own emotions and maintaining a sense of clarity in times of crisis, they were able to effectively guide their troops through turbulent and uncertain conditions.

In unambiguous contrast to the steady, composed leader is the bad General, who buckles under pressure and makes decisions that exacerbate the crisis at hand. Bad Generals often struggle with decision-making in times of uncertainty, allowing fear, ego, or panic to cloud their judgment. Their inability to remain calm and focused leads to rash, irrational decisions that further destabilise the situation and create additional chaos.

One of the key challenges that bad Generals face during crises is their tendency to react impulsively rather than respond with careful thought and deliberation. In their desperation to regain control of the situation, they may make hasty decisions that undermine their position, damage morale, or worsen the conflict.

This can result in a cascade of poor choices, each compounding the last, until the crisis spirals out of control.

A historical example of this is the leadership of General Robert E. Lee during the American Civil War. Although Lee is often lauded for his military prowess, there were several instances during the war where his decision-making under crisis led to unnecessary losses. One such example occurred during the Battle of Gettysburg in 1863, where Lee made several key decisions, such as the ill-fated Pickett's Charge, that resulted in heavy Confederate casualties and ultimately led to the retreat of his forces. Lee's overconfidence and failure to adapt to changing circumstances on the battlefield contributed to his army's defeat, highlighting the dangers of irrational decision-making in times of crisis.

General George McClellan, who commanded Union forces early in the Civil War, was often criticised for his hesitancy and lack of decisiveness during critical moments. McClellan's inability to act decisively during the Peninsula Campaign of 1862 resulted in missed opportunities to strike a decisive blow against the Coalition. His fear of taking risks and his tendency to overestimate the strength of the enemy led to a prolonged conflict, contributing to unnecessary casualties and delays in achieving Union objectives. McClellan's leadership failures in times of crisis ultimately led to his removal from command, but his inability to handle pressure had lasting consequences on the course of the war.

The inability to make sound decisions during moments of crisis is not limited to historical examples. In modern military leadership, bad Generals who fail to manage stress and uncertainty can have similarly disastrous consequences. During the wars in Iraq and Afghanistan, for example, some commanders struggled to navigate complex and evolving battlefield conditions. Their inability to adapt to changing circumstances, combined with poor communication and leadership during moments of crisis, led to significant setbacks and casualties.

History is full of military leaders who have succeeded or failed in times of crisis, offering valuable lessons for today's and future leaders.

One of the most instructive examples is the leadership of Winston Churchill during World War II. Churchill's leadership during the darkest days of the war, particularly during the Battle of Britain, exemplified the power of steadfast resolve and strategic vision during a time of overwhelming crisis. With the British Islands facing the threat of Nazi invasion, Churchill remained unflinching in his resolve, rallying the British people with his famous speeches and unwavering commitment to victory. His ability to navigate the crisis, both politically and militarily, was instrumental in securing Britain's survival and ultimately contributing to the Allied victory in Europe.

General George S. Patton, whose leadership during World War II was characterised by his boldness and decisiveness. Patton's aggressive tactics and willingness to take calculated risks allowed him to successfully navigate crises on the battlefield, from the Sicily Campaign of 1943 to the Battle of the Bulge in December 1944 to January 1945. Patton's ability to inspire his troops and make quick, decisive decisions during moments of uncertainty was key to the success of the Allied forces in Europe. His leadership style, while controversial at times, demonstrated the importance of confidence and clarity during times of crisis.

However, not all historical leaders were able to navigate crises successfully, and the failures of bad Generals offer important lessons about the dangers of poor leadership under pressure.

THE VERY VERY BEST BAD 4-STAR GENERAL

One of the most catastrophic examples of leadership failure during a crisis can be found in the leadership of Napoleon Bonaparte during the Russian campaign of 1812. Napoleon, who had previously enjoyed remarkable success on the battlefield, faced an unprecedented crisis during his invasion of Russia. Overconfidence, poor decision-making, and an inability to adapt to the harsh Russian winter led to a devastating retreat and the loss of nearly his entire army. Napoleon's failure to manage the crisis not only resulted in the destruction of his forces but also marked the beginning of his downfall.

One of the key takeaways from these examples is the importance of adaptability in crisis leadership. Successful leaders understand that crises are fluid, unpredictable events that require the ability to think on one's feet, adapt strategies in real-time, and make decisions based on evolving circumstances. A good leader is not wedded to a rigid plan but is flexible enough to adjust to changing conditions. This adaptability allows leaders to maintain control in the midst of chaos, manage uncertainty, and ultimately guide their forces to success.

Moreover, effective crisis leaders understand that failure to adapt and learn from past experiences can have disastrous consequences. Good Generals seek to learn from their mistakes and failures, using these lessons to refine their leadership approach and enhance their decision-making abilities in future crises. This commitment to continuous learning is a symbol of effective leadership, ensuring that leaders are better equipped to handle the challenges of future crises.

Conclusively, crisis is an inevitable part of military leadership, and the way a leader navigates these moments of uncertainty and stress can have a profound impact on the outcome of a conflict. The best Generals remain calm, focused, and decisive in times of crisis, inspiring confidence in their troops and guiding them toward success.

In contrast, bad Generals who struggle under pressure often make irrational decisions that exacerbate the crisis, leading to further conflict and failure. Through the lessons of history, we can see that the ability to manage chaos and uncertainty is not only a test of a leader's character but also a determinant of military success or failure. As such, effective leadership in times of crisis is a critical component of military strategy, one that can shape the course of history and determine the fate of nations.

*

CHAPTER 19

REBUILDING AFTER FAILURE: LEADERSHIP IN THE AFTERMATH OF DEFEAT

Failure, especially in military leadership, can be a deeply humbling experience. It is during these times, after a significant setback or defeat, that a leader's true character is tested. While victory often gathers attention and praise, it is how a leader handles failure, both personally and organisationally, that ultimately defines their legacy. Good leaders understand that failure is not an endpoint but an opportunity for reflection, growth, and rebuilding. They recognise the importance of maintaining morale, learning from their mistakes, and charting a new path forward for their forces.

In contrast, bad Generals often fail to take responsibility for failure, opting instead for scapegoating, denial, or shifting blame. This chapter explores the critical role of leadership in the aftermath of defeat, focusing on how great Generals rebuild their forces and regain trust, while ineffective leaders perpetuate failure by failing to learn from their mistakes.

Military defeat is inevitable for any force, as even the best-laid plans can fail due to strategy, logistics, miscommunication, overconfidence, or luck. True leadership is measured not by failure itself, but by the response to it.

THE VERY VERY BEST BAD 4-STAR GENERAL

When the military force suffers defeat, it often faces a combination of practical and psychological challenges. The practical challenges include rebuilding military capabilities, restoring strategic momentum, and securing essential resources. However, the psychological challenges are often far more insidious. Soldiers may lose confidence in their leaders, morale may fall, and the *esprit de corps* of the unit may disintegrate. In such circumstances, it is the leader's role to restore faith in the mission, rebuild trust, and guide their forces through the emotional aftermath of defeat.

The symbol of a great military leader is the ability to take responsibility for setbacks and guide their forces through the process of rebuilding. Strong leaders view failure as an opportunity for learning and growth. Rather than blaming others, they own their mistakes and use them as a foundation for future success. Equally, they understand the importance of restoring morale and confidence within their ranks. When soldiers witness leaders taking responsibility, they are inspired to follow with renewed commitment and trust.

A prime example of such leadership comes from General Winston Churchill during World War II. Churchill's leadership after the early defeats of the war, such as the fall of France and the evacuation of Dunkirk, was instrumental in maintaining Britain's resolve. In the face of these early setbacks, Churchill never wavered in his belief that Britain could prevail. Rather than shifting blame or retreating into denial, he used these defeats to rally the British people and military forces, turning these failures into a source of determination. His speeches, such as the famous *"We shall fight on the beaches"* speech, not only restored hope but also inspired a sense of collective responsibility and national unity. In addition to his public resolve, Churchill focused on rebuilding the military and forging stronger alliances.

He was quick to reorganise the military leadership, appointing capable officers who could effectively lead the war effort. Churchill understood the importance of learning from mistakes, and he demanded that his Generals assess their failures and develop strategies to prevent similar issues in the future. Through his leadership, Britain was able to recover from early defeats and ultimately emerge victorious.

Another example of a leader who successfully rebuilt after failure is General George S. Patton during World War II. Patton's leadership in the aftermath of the setbacks suffered by the Allies in North Africa is a testament to his resilience. After the initial difficulties in the North African campaign, Patton took command of the U.S. II Corps and quickly turned the tide of the campaign. He instilled discipline, demanded excellence, and ensured that his troops understood the importance of their role in the broader strategic context.

Patton's emphasis on aggressive tactics and his ability to rebuild his forces after defeat were key to the eventual success in North Africa and Italy. Patton also demonstrated the importance of psychological leadership after failure. He knew that the recovery from a military defeat was not just about reorganising forces or refining tactics but also about rebuilding the morale of the troops. His speeches, while sometimes controversial, were designed to inspire confidence and unity in his soldiers. Patton's ability to rally his troops after setbacks was a critical factor in his success as a military leader.

In contrast, bad Generals often fail to take ownership of their failures. Instead of confronting the reasons behind the defeat, they engage in scapegoating, deny their responsibility, or attempt to shift blame onto subordinates or external factors. This failure to acknowledge their mistakes results in a lack of trust from their troops and a perpetuation of failure. When a leader refuses to learn from defeat, the organisation stagnates and morale declines, making recovery even more difficult.

One of the most glaring examples of such behaviour comes from the leadership of General Sir Douglas Haig during World War I. Haig, who commanded British forces on the Western Front, was frequently criticised for his failure to adapt his strategies after the devastating losses of the Battle of the Somme and other engagements. Rather than taking ownership of his mistakes or reassessing his strategies, Haig continued with the same tactics that had already led to unnecessary casualties and little strategic gain. His refusal to acknowledge the limits of his approach and his continued focus on attrition-based warfare led to widespread disillusionment within the ranks.

Haig's failure to adjust to changing conditions and his refusal to take responsibility for the failure of his tactics ultimately had disastrous consequences. His leadership in the aftermath of these defeats did little to inspire confidence in his troops, and the army remained bogged down in a protracted and futile conflict. Haig's inability to adapt, take ownership of mistakes, and rebuild after defeat is one of the many reasons why his leadership is often considered a failure in the annals of military history.

Similarly, in more recent history, the leadership of General William Westmoreland during the Vietnam War provides an example of a leader who struggled to adapt to the realities of warfare and failed to take responsibility for defeat. Westmoreland, who commanded U.S. forces in Vietnam from 1964 to 1968, was criticised for his rigid adherence to conventional military tactics, which were ill-suited to the guerrilla warfare tactics employed by the Viet Cong. Despite mounting casualties and a failure to achieve a decisive victory, Westmoreland continued to pursue a strategy of attrition, which further exacerbated the situation. His inability to reassess his strategy or acknowledge the failure of his tactics contributed to the eventual withdrawal of U.S. forces and the defeat in Vietnam. Westmoreland's inability to accept responsibility for the failure of his strategy resulted in a lack of accountability within the U.S. military leadership. This failure to confront the realities of the war and make necessary adjustments left the troops demoralised and contributed to the eventual loss of the war. Westmoreland's leadership after the defeat was marked by denial, miscommunication, and a lack of transparency, all of which compounded the failure and prolonged the crisis.

The ability to learn from mistakes is one of the most important qualities of a good military leader. A leader who takes responsibility for their failures and seeks to understand the reasons behind those failures is far more likely to succeed in the future. Conversely, a leader who refuses to learn from mistakes is doomed to repeat them. The process of rebuilding after failure involves not just restoring military strength but also critically examining the decisions and strategies that led to the setback.

For example, after the defeat at the Battle of the Little Bighorn in 1876, where General George Armstrong Custer and his forces were decimated by Native American tribes, the U.S. military learned valuable lessons that would inform future campaigns. While Custer's failure was a result of his overconfidence and tactical mistakes, the military as a whole learned the importance of proper reconnaissance, understanding the enemy, and the need for coordination between various military units. This learning process, though painful, contributed to future successes in the Indian Wars.

Similarly, after the failure of Operation Market Garden during World War II, the Allies took time to reflect on the lessons of the operation. Despite the initial setbacks, military leaders acknowledged the flaws in the planning and execution of the operation and took steps to prevent similar mistakes in the future. The ability to learn from failure was crucial to the success of future Allied campaigns, particularly in the months leading up to the D-Day invasion.

Rebuilding morale and trust after defeat is perhaps the most critical aspect of leadership in the aftermath of failure. Soldiers are often deeply affected by the emotional and psychological toll of defeat, and a leader must be able to provide reassurance, instil confidence, and inspire a renewed sense of purpose. Good leaders understand that their troops look to them for guidance, especially after a failure, and they must provide the support necessary to rebuild trust in the leadership and the mission.

General Dwight D. Eisenhower, in his role as Supreme Commander of the Allied Expeditionary Force, understood the importance of morale in rebuilding after defeat. Following the failure of Operation Market Garden, Eisenhower addressed the soldiers and reaffirmed their commitment to the broader mission of defeating Nazi Germany. He acknowledged the difficulties of the operation but focused on the long-term goals of the campaign. Eisenhower's leadership helped maintain morale and unity within the Allied forces, enabling them to regroup and continue the fight.

Conclusively, the aftermath of military defeat is a critical moment for leadership. The best Generals understand that failure is not an end but an opportunity to reflect, rebuild, and learn. They take ownership of their mistakes, restore morale, and lead their forces forward with renewed determination. In contrast, bad Generals who refuse to accept responsibility for failure or engage in scapegoating risk perpetuating the cycle of failure.

The ability to rebuild after defeat is one of the most important qualities of a great leader, and history provides numerous examples of leaders who succeeded by learning from their mistakes and rebuilding their forces. By studying these examples, we can gain valuable insights into the nature of military leadership and the critical role that leadership plays in times of adversity.

CHAPTER 20

THE MORAL COMPASS OF COMMAND: INTEGRITY VERSUS EXPEDIENCY

Military leadership is a vessel in which the courage of a General is tested, often in the most difficult of circumstances. When stakes are high, commanders face a moral dilemma: uphold their values at the cost of immediate success or choose convenience for tactical gain. This tension between integrity and expediency is perhaps most evident in the heat of battle, where lives are at stake, and the consequences of decisions can resonate for years, if not decades.

The best Generals are those who, despite the mounting pressures of war, maintain their moral compass and remain true to their ethical principles. They understand that the long-term integrity of the military and the well-being of their soldiers outweigh short-term gains. In contrast, bad Generals may compromise their values for immediate success, only to find that the cost of such decisions is far greater than any tactical victory they might have achieved.

Military conflict is inherently fraught with moral challenges. Decisions are often made under extreme stress, with limited time for reflection and the potential for grave consequences.

In these high-stakes situations, the temptation to choose the convenient option, one that promises an immediate and tangible result, is powerful. However, this can come at a steep moral cost, particularly when it involves sacrificing the well-being of soldiers, violating international laws, or disregarding ethical principles.

A good leader understands that the long-term effects of these decisions are far-reaching. Even a seemingly small moral compromise can erode trust and cohesion within the ranks. This damages the reputation of the military institution and tarnishes the honour of the leader who makes these decisions. It can also have devastating consequences for the civilian population, international relations, and the broader sense of justice. For these reasons, the best Generals stick to their ethical principles, even when doing so risks the immediate success of a mission.

In contrast, bad Generals often make decisions driven by pragmatism, sacrificing integrity for perceived expediency. They may resort to unethical tactics, lie to their troops or superiors, or justify morally questionable decisions as necessary for the greater good. However, these decisions often lead to catastrophic consequences, both in the short term and in the long run. The damage to morale, trust, and the reputation of the military institution can be irreversible. Furthermore, bad Generals may find that the tactical successes gained through unethical means are fleeting and hollow, as they fail to consider the broader implications of their actions.

Integrity is a cornerstone of military leadership. Soldiers place their trust in their commanders, and that trust is built on a foundation of honesty, honour, and ethical conduct. A General who demonstrates integrity commands respect, inspires loyalty, and fosters an environment where soldiers can perform at their best. Integrity ensures that the leader's decisions align with both the values of the military institution and the broader moral codes of society.

This includes the rules of engagement, international humanitarian law, and the protection of civilians.

One of the most important aspects of integrity is the leader's ability to be transparent and honest with their troops. This involves taking responsibility for mistakes, acknowledging the challenges of a mission, and setting clear, ethical expectations for conduct. In battle, when the fog of war clouds, judgment and emotions run high, a leader's unwavering commitment to ethical principles becomes a guiding light for their soldiers, helping them to stay grounded and focused on the larger mission. This is even when the immediate situation seems overwhelming. Moreover, integrity requires consistency. A good leader demonstrates the same ethical principles in peacetime as they do in times of conflict. This consistency not only builds trust but also ensures that the leader's actions align with their words, reinforcing the moral fabric of the military institution.

While integrity fosters trust, the pursuit of expediency often erodes it. Generals who prioritise short-term tactical advantages at the expense of ethical principles may achieve immediate success, but they risk undermining the cohesion and morale of their forces. In the long run, such decisions create a toxic environment where the values of the military institution are compromised, and soldiers are forced to reconcile their loyalty to a leader with their own personal ethics.

One of the most notable examples of the dangers of expediency is the leadership of General William Westmoreland during the Vietnam War. Westmoreland, who commanded U.S. forces in Vietnam from 1964 to 1968, faced mounting pressure to show progress in a war that was becoming increasingly unpopular and difficult. To justify the continued U.S. involvement and secure political support, Westmoreland and his subordinates were accused of manipulating intelligence reports and inflating body counts in order to create the appearance of success.

This attempt to portray a false narrative was driven by expediency: the need to maintain morale at home, reassure political leaders, and justify the cost of the war.

However, the decision to prioritise expediency over integrity had far-reaching consequences. The manipulation of intelligence not only eroded trust within the military but also further alienated the American public. It became increasingly clear that the U.S. was not winning the war, and the dishonesty of the leadership compounded the disillusionment felt by both soldiers and civilians. The ultimate result of Westmoreland's leadership was not only a defeat in Vietnam but also a deepening of the moral and ethical rift between the military and the broader society. The failure to uphold integrity during the conflict contributed to the erosion of confidence in military leadership. The expedient decisions made at the highest levels of command left lasting scars on both the U.S. Army and the American public.

Personal Stories

There are numerous examples in history of military leaders who faced critical decisions and chose integrity, even when it meant risking success. One of the most famous examples is that of General Dwight D. Eisenhower during World War II. Eisenhower, who was tasked with overseeing the D-Day invasion, faced a moral dilemma in the days leading up to the operation. The weather conditions were uncertain, and there was a significant risk involved in proceeding with the invasion. Some of his advisers urged him to delay the operation, but Eisenhower chose to proceed, believing that the moral imperative to liberate Europe outweighed the potential costs of failure. Eisenhower's decision to maintain his integrity, even under tremendous pressure, had a profound impact on the success of the mission. Despite the risks, the invasion went forward, and it became one of the most significant turning points of the war.

THE VERY VERY BEST BAD 4-STAR GENERAL

Eisenhower's ability to stick to his principles, even when the odds were stacked against him, inspired his soldiers and allies alike, reinforcing the importance of ethical leadership in moments of crisis.

Another example of ethical leadership comes from General Omar Bradley, who served as the commander of U.S. forces in Europe during World War II. Bradley was known for his integrity and his ability to make difficult decisions based on moral principles. One of the most significant moments in his leadership came during the battle for the French city of Saint-Lô. This is when Bradley had to decide whether to launch a risky attack that could potentially result in massive casualties. Despite the pressure to act quickly and achieve a victory, Bradley chose to proceed with caution, carefully considering the risks to his soldiers. His decision to prioritise the welfare of his troops over the expediency of a quick victory was a testament to his commitment to ethical leadership.

The consequences of compromising one's integrity for expediency can be catastrophic, both for the leader and for the military. While the immediate tactical advantage may seem worth the moral cost, the long-term repercussions are often more damaging. When a leader compromises their principles, they create a culture of dishonesty and corruption within their forces. Soldiers may begin to question the ethical standards of their leaders and may be less inclined to follow orders that conflict with their moral beliefs. Over time, this erosion of trust can lead to a breakdown in military discipline, a loss of mission focus, and a deterioration of the moral foundation upon which the military institution is built.

In contrast, when a leader upholds their ethical principles, even in the face of adversity, they inspire loyalty, respect, and trust. Their actions set a standard for the entire military, demonstrating that success is not measured solely by victories on the battlefield but also by the integrity of the forces that fight. The long-term impact of such leadership is profound, as it strengthens the moral fabric of the military and ensures that future generations of soldiers are guided by principles that transcend the immediate demands of war.

Conclusively, the moral compass of military leadership is a delicate balance between integrity and expediency. Good Generals understand that the ethical decisions they make, particularly in the heat of battle, have far-reaching consequences. They make difficult choices that prioritise ethics over short-term gains, knowing long-term success and the military's reputation depend on it. In contrast, bad Generals often compromise their values for expediency, only to find that the consequences of such decisions are far more damaging than any tactical victory. The history of military leadership is rich with examples of leaders who faced moral dilemmas and chose integrity, as well as those who compromised their values for the sake of expediency. These decisions shape the future of both the military and the broader society as they provide valuable lessons for leaders today and in the future.

*

CHAPTER 21

TRANSFORMING LEADERSHIP: LESSONS FOR THE FUTURE

Leadership is never static. It evolves with the times, guided by past lessons, present challenges, and future vision. This is especially in the military, where leadership directly impacts soldiers, missions, and national security. In an era defined by rapid technological advancements, shifting geopolitical realities, and increasingly complex threats, the role of the military leader has become more demanding than ever. Victory is no longer determined solely by battlefield tactics or the weight of firepower.

Today's leaders must navigate political intricacies, lead diverse teams, integrate emerging technologies and confront unconventional threats. To thrive in this environment, military leadership must undergo transformation. This includes moving from rigid, transactional models to adaptive, visionary, and ethically grounded approaches. This transformation requires both learning from the triumphs and failures of the past. This fosters the qualities that will define future success, adaptability, integrity, inclusivity, innovation, and emotional intelligence.

Traditional leadership models are anchored in hierarchy, authority, and discipline. They remain essential to maintain order and operational effectiveness. However, on their own, they are insufficient for the complexities of modern warfare. Transformational leadership goes beyond giving orders and enforcing compliance; it inspires people to rise above self-interest, work for a shared purpose, and embrace change.

Transformational leaders are visionaries who empower others, nurture trust, and create a culture where adaptability and ethical decision-making are paramount. They recognise that modern military success depends as much on the ability to unite and inspire diverse teams as it does on strategy and logistics. They balance authority with empathy, decisiveness with openness, and tradition with innovation.

The future of military leadership cannot be built in isolation from history. Studying both the achievements and failures of past commanders provides invaluable guidance for avoiding pitfalls and replicating success. History honours leaders who combined humility with strategic vision. By embracing the humility of great leaders and rejecting the rigidity of failed ones, emerging commanders can chart a new course rooted in the enduring principles of integrity, respect, and responsibility, yet responsive to the demands of a changing world.

Transforming leadership is not a matter of rhetoric; it demands deliberate systemic change.

The following pillars outline the foundation for a stronger, more resilient military leadership culture.

Leadership development at every stage

From the moment a soldier enters service, leadership training should be embedded alongside tactical and physical instruction. This includes ethical decision-making and the skills to inspire and guide others.

Mentorship is central to this process. Pairing emerging leaders with experienced mentors allows wisdom to be passed on, fosters humility, and provides a sounding board for navigating complex challenges. This approach prevents the arrogance and isolation that often derail promising careers.

Emotional intelligence and empathy

Leaders who understand their own emotions and those of their subordinates are better equipped to maintain morale and cohesion under pressure. Emotional intelligence fosters loyalty, trust, and a shared sense of purpose. By creating an environment where soldiers feel valued and understood, leaders strengthen not only the individual but the unit as a whole. Empathy does not weaken discipline; it reinforces commitment and resilience.

Open communication and transparency

While discipline demands clear chains of command, effective leadership also requires two-way communication. Leaders should actively listen, seek feedback, and explain the rationale behind their decisions. Transparency builds trust. When soldiers understand the "*why*" behind orders, they execute with greater conviction, reducing friction and fostering unity.

Diversity and inclusion as strategic assets

A modern fighting force is strengthened by the variety of perspectives, skills, and experiences its members bring. Leaders who embrace diversity harness greater creativity, problem-solving capacity, and adaptability. Inclusivity is not a moral gesture; it is a strategic advantage. Leaders must dismantle barriers to equal opportunity, combat bias, and ensure that every soldier feels they have a place and purpose in the mission.

Innovation and adaptability

The battlefield is constantly changing. Leaders must be willing to question outdated methods, encourage creative problem-solving, and embrace new technologies. An environment that supports calculated risks and treats failures as learning opportunities keeps the force agile and prepared for the unexpected. This may be a cyber-attack, a humanitarian crisis, or an unconventional conflict.

Integrity and accountability

The bedrock of military leadership is integrity. Leaders must embody the standards they demand of others; being honest, ethical, and accountable, even when it is difficult. Mistakes are inevitable; covering them up is inexcusable. Leaders who admit errors and take responsibility earn lasting respect, while those who deflect blame erode trust.

The challenges of the future technological disruption, shifting alliances, and asymmetric threats demand leaders who are both principled and adaptable. The military of tomorrow will require commanders who can unite diverse teams, integrate innovation seamlessly into operations, and uphold the highest ethical standards under pressure. This transformation will not happen overnight. It will require emerging leaders to challenge the status quo, commit to lifelong learning, and consciously shape the culture of their institutions. It will require courage not only in battle, but in the boardroom, in moments of moral decision, and in the face of resistance to change.

Conclusively, the transformation of military leadership is not optional; it is essential for survival and success in the modern era. By studying the past with clear eyes, embracing diversity, fostering innovation, leading with empathy, and holding fast to integrity, emerging leaders can build armed forces that are resilient, unified, and ready for the unknown. The leaders of tomorrow must be more than commanders; they must be visionaries, mentors, and guardians of the values that make a military a force for good. In doing so, they will ensure that, no matter how unpredictable the world becomes, the armed forces remain steadfast, disciplined in purpose, adaptable in strategy, and unwavering in honour.

*

CHAPTER 22

THE FINAL SALUTE – A RECKONING WITH POWER, INTEGRITY, AND ENDURING PATRIOTISM

Every great institution faces a moment when leadership is tested, not by battle, but by the dangers of unchecked power and the cost of trading honour for personal gain. For example, a senior military figure who won't be mentioned here rose to prominence but fell into controversy. This shows the dangers of treating leadership as an idol rather than a responsibility. At the height of his command, this leader displayed traits that initially evoked surprise. But as time wore on.

Those close to the core of military life began to witness a chilling transformation. Rather than stepping down when the call of duty had been fulfilled, he tenaciously clung to power. Not out of vision, not to groom successors, but out of fear; fear of losing relevance, fear of retribution, and most curiously, fear rooted in superstition.

Belief in supernatural protection, commonly referred to in African society as muti, found a troubling place in leadership decision-making. Command choices were no longer guided by principle, logic, or national interest. Instead, rituals and advisors outside the chain of military accountability began to influence operational and personnel decisions. Trust in the leadership diminished.

THE VERY VERY BEST BAD 4-STAR GENERAL

Confidence among junior officers and troops began to erode, as discipline gave way to confusion and suspicion. The consequences were devastating. Morale, the invisible fuel that drives any military force, dropped to dangerous levels. The once-proud spirit of service began to fade. Officers who had given their lives to study, sacrifice, and duty watched as promotions became tools of favouritism. Deployment decisions were no longer based on capability, but on loyalty to an individual rather than allegiance to the nation or the sovereign. The chain of command, once sacred, became a web of whispered fears and cautious navigation.

The senior figure's refusal to relinquish power did more than just stunt the institution's growth, it weaponised stagnation. Young leaders with potential were sidelined. Merit-based advancement became a remnant of the past. The military became an echo chamber, recycling broken leadership ideas under the illusion of continuity. As the troops grew disheartened, their sense of purpose was replaced with survivalism. Yet, from the cracks in this dark season, valuable light emerges for those willing to see.

Every oppressive season births a lesson, and this one is no exception. Those who lived through the moral decline now possess a unique advantage from which to guide the future. For leadership is not defined by rank, age, or years of service, but by the courage to do what is right, even when it is unpopular, and the humility to step aside when your time has passed.

The measure of a true leader is not in how long they hold on to power, but in how they steward it, how they pass it on, and how they prepare the institution for a future without them. Clinging to authority out of fear or superstition breeds rot; releasing it in wisdom and faith cultivates legacy.

Those who survive such corrupt seasons often do so in silence, under immense pressure, and sometimes in complete isolation, but their solitude is not in vain. It is within that silence that integrity is fortified. It is during those years in the shadows that character is sharpened. One must never mistake being overlooked for being unworthy. Sometimes, the most principled officers are those intentionally kept far from the spotlight, because their presence is a threat to the impure.

To those future leaders who read this, stay rooted. Patriotism is not defined by proximity to power, but by your unwavering commitment to your nation and your values, even when the system seems broken. Develop yourself continuously, study and observe. Remain sober in thought and strong in spirit. Do not fall into the same trap of pursuing influence at the expense of your soul. Do not use culture or spiritual manipulation as a substitute for competence and courage. Let the past be your compass.

The military must reclaim its moral backbone, not just with discipline and order, but with vision, humility, and ethical conviction. Officers must no longer be moulded by fear or favouritism, but by excellence and sacrifice. The time has come for a new generation of leaders who can rise without bitterness, command without corruption, and salute the flag with a heart that beats for the nation, not personal gain.

As the final pages of this book close, let it serve not only as a chronicle of the past but as a warning and a beacon. Institutions can fall, but they can also rise again. The future rests not in those who hold power for too long, but in those willing to lead with integrity and let go when the mission is done. Let this be the final salute, not to a man, but to the principle that leadership must be earned, exercised with wisdom, and surrendered with honour.

*

CHAPTER 23

WHO WILL LEAD US?

As the world evolves at an unprecedented pace, so too must the leaders tasked with guiding the forces that defend and protect us. Throughout this book, we have examined the intricate degrees of military leadership, the blunt contrasts between effective and ineffective Generals, and the profound impact leadership has on the success or failure of military institutions. The decisions made by Generals influence not only the outcomes of wars and conflicts but the future direction of nations, the welfare of their people, and the very integrity of their armed forces.

As we conclude this exploration, we are left with one fundamental question: who will lead us? Also, more importantly, how will they lead us? The future of military leadership, especially in the face of increasingly complex and dynamic challenges, depends on a combination of visionary foresight, ethical commitment, and an understanding of the needs of both soldiers and society. This chapter seeks to offer a final reflection on the responsibilities of military leaders, with an emphasis on the paramount importance of ethical leadership, service to the people, and the long-term implications of the decisions made in times of war and peace.

THE VERY VERY BEST BAD 4-STAR GENERAL

At its core, a General's role extends beyond strategy and battlefield decisions to leading and inspiring people. The General must foster trust, discipline, and morale, mentor the next generation of leaders, and uphold the military's values of honour, respect, and ethical conduct.

While battlefield decisions are critical, it is daily leadership that truly shapes an army's success. The culture a General creates, whether one of integrity and professionalism or favouritism and fear, leaves a legacy long after the battle ends. Generals' responsibilities also extend to society, as the trust and legitimacy of the military are crucial for civil-military relations. A respected and ethical military strengthens national stability, whereas leaders who ignore these responsibilities risk alienating the very people they serve.

Throughout this book, we have seen military leaders who upheld ethical standards and those who succumbed to expediency, corruption, or self-interest. The lesson is clear: ethical leadership is essential. A General must serve the people and act morally, even under pressure. Ethical leadership forms the foundation of a healthy, effective military. It ensures decisions prioritise the well-being of soldiers, the nation's interests, and justice, rather than personal gain. Leaders who remain true to their principles inspire loyalty, trust, and a culture of integrity throughout the institution. Such leaders recognise the long-term impact of their actions. Compromising values may yield short-term gains, but it risks lasting damage to morale and credibility. History shows that when ethical standards erode, corruption and institutional failure follow. To remain respected and effective, ethical leadership must guide every level of command.

Looking ahead, military leadership faces unprecedented challenges. Rapid technological advancement, complex global conflicts, and non-traditional warfare. This demands leaders who are adaptable, innovative, and forward-thinking.

The military is no longer just a fighting force; it is a dynamic institution engaging governments, corporations, and international organisations. Leaders must navigate the intersection of technology, diplomacy, and warfare. This is to ensure their forces remain capable while upholding ethical responsibilities. Future Generals will need to integrate emerging technologies with traditional strategies, remaining flexible and prepared to evolve as conflicts change. They must also anticipate ethical dilemmas and risks associated with these innovations. Moreover, leaders must foster an inclusive and diverse military, attracting and developing talent from varied backgrounds. Diversity will be a core strength, requiring leaders to dismantle barriers, combat discrimination, and create environments where all soldiers are valued and empowered.

While the General's primary duty may be to command and protect their forces, their ultimate responsibility lies with the people they serve. Generals are entrusted with the protection of a nation's citizens, and their actions must always reflect this sacred responsibility. Military leadership is not about wielding power; it is about serving the greater good of society. The military exists not for the benefit of its officers or leaders but to protect the sovereignty and security of the nation, preserve peace, and ensure that the values of society are upheld.

Generals must be deeply connected to the society they serve, understanding the challenges and aspirations of the people. Their leadership must reflect the broader values of justice, democracy, and human rights.

In times of peace, this means engaging with civilian leaders, promoting stability, and ensuring that the military's actions are aligned with the needs and desires of the population. In times of conflict, this means maintaining the highest standards of conduct, minimising harm to civilians, and striving to resolve conflicts through diplomacy and negotiation when possible.

The Generals who view themselves as servants of the people will lead with humility, empathy, and a sense of moral responsibility. They will understand that their authority is not derived from their rank or position but from their duty to serve and protect the people who have entrusted them with their security.

The absence of effective, ethical leadership can have devastating consequences, both for the military and the broader society. When military leaders fail to uphold their responsibilities, the results can be catastrophic. The erosion of trust, the loss of morale, and the breakdown of discipline within the ranks can have far-reaching consequences, undermining national security and stability. Bad leadership can fuel corruption, foster divisions within the military, and even lead to internal rebellions or coups.

Moreover, the consequences of poor leadership extend beyond the military itself. When a nation's military is led by Generals who lack integrity or vision, the entire social fabric can be affected. Trust in public institutions erodes, civil-military relations become strained, and the very security of the nation can be compromised. A failure of leadership in the military can set off a chain reaction that destabilises the broader political system and undermines the welfare of the nation's citizens. Thus, the responsibility of Generals is not only to their troops but also to the nation. They must act with foresight, wisdom, and ethical integrity, understanding that their decisions affect not just the battlefield but the broader social and political order.

Conclusively, as we consider the future of military leadership, the question remains, *"Who will lead us?"* The answer lies not in the Generals of today, but in the leaders of tomorrow. The next generation of military leaders must be prepared to meet the challenges of an increasingly complex world. They must be adaptable, visionary, and deeply committed to ethical leadership.

To build a military that is truly capable of meeting the challenges of the future, we must invest in developing leaders. Leaders who understand the importance of integrity, who are committed to service to the people, and who are willing to learn from both the mistakes and successes of the past. These leaders must not only be capable of commanding troops on the battlefield but also of navigating the complex and often dangerous terrain of global politics, technology, and society.

The future of military leadership depends on those who are willing to step forward, take responsibility, and lead with honour, humility, and commitment to justice. The Generals of tomorrow must understand that their ultimate duty is not to their own ambitions or their own power, but to the service of the people and the protection of the values that make a nation strong. As we look to the future, we can only hope that the next generation of military leaders will rise to the challenge. They will build a new era of leadership that is characterised by integrity, service, and a deep commitment to the welfare of the nation and its people.

*

THE VERY VERY BEST BAD 4-STAR GENERAL

AUTHOR BIOGRAPHY

Olly Peter Nyirenda is a seasoned military officer and strategic thinker from the Kingdom of Eswatini. He is a graduate and alumnus of the Botswana Defence Force – Force Training Establishment (BDF FTE), Military Training Establishment of Zambia (MILTEZ), Zimbabwe Staff College, South African Defence Intelligence College (SADIC), South African National Defence Force College of Education and Technology (SANDF COLET), Defence Services Command and Staff College – Zambia, and the prestigious National Defence University in Washington, D.C., under the Africa Center for Strategic Studies.

His distinguished career in the Umbutfo Eswatini Defence Force and His Majesty's Correctional Services, where he helped establish the Intelligence Unit includes a broad range of appointments; rifleman, battalion clerk, platoon commander, unit adjutant, company commander, battalion second-in-command, desk officer intelligence, training officer intelligence, director military intelligence, officer commanding advance training wing, senior staff officer doctrine, and staff officer grade two research and development.

Regionally, he has contributed to SADC's collective security through participation in the multinational peace support training, Exercise Thokgamo, Exercise Southern Accord 14 under U.S. Africa Command, and as a member of the SADC intelligence community training task team responsible for drafting the SADC Intelligence Training Doctrine.

As a devoted patriot and scholar-practitioner, Nyirenda is known for his principled stand, unwavering loyalty to the monarchy, and dedication to inspiring a new generation of military leaders and public servants.

THE VERY VERY BEST BAD 4-STAR GENERAL

www.ingramcontent.com/pod-product-compliance
Lightning Source LLC
Chambersburg PA
CBHW052100230426
43662CB00036B/1719